VITRUVIUS
DEDHAMENSIS

QVINQVE

LIBRI

ARCHI-

TECT-

VRAE

MCMXCII
AD

Architectural Monographs No 27

QUINLAN TERRY
SELECTED WORKS

A.D. ACADEMY EDITIONS

Architectural Monographs No 27
Editorial Offices
42 Leinster Gardens London W2 3AN

ISSN 0141-2191

Editorial and Design Team
Andreas Papadakis (Publisher)
Richard Economakis (Editorial)
Andrea Bettella (Senior Designer)
Owen Thomas, John Honderich

Subscription Department
Mira Joka
42 Leinster Gardens London W2 3AN

Credits
Quinlan Terry's knowledge of Classical architecture was gained through 11 years working experience with Raymond Erith until his death in 1973. Erith was the sort of architect who designed everything himself and delegated little. He therefore had a small staff and refused commissions which he was not able to carry out personally. Quinlan Terry continued in that same tradition, never employing more than 12 assistants. Even so, an appreciation of his work is not complete without acknowledging the debt he owes to those in his office whose practical experience of building, working knowledge and diligence have been invaluable. First among these is Hugh Barrell who started working for Raymond Erith in 1947; without his constant attention to detail both in the office and on site, many of the projects would not have been completed satisfactorily. Also Edward Dale, who joined the firm in 1968 and who managed the greater part of the contractual work on Richmond Riverside, has given essential and constant assistance.

Photography
Photographs are reproduced by kind permission of the following: Nick Carter pp 2, 66, 67, 69, 70-77, 113 (top), 114-118, 122; Charles Hall pp 36, 37, 40, 41, 43, 44, 46-49, 55, 58, 59, 78 (top), 104, 105, 113 (bottom), 119; Mark Fiennes pp 39, 78 (bottom), 79, 86; Derry Moore, courtesy of *Architectural Digest*, pp 56, 57, 68; Timothy Soar pp 60, 61 (bottom left), 88, 106, 107, 108, 109; Tim Imrie, courtesy of © *Country Life*, p 61 (bottom right); Bruce Van Inwegan, courtesy of *Architectural Digest* © 1989 Architectural Digest Publishing Corp. All rights reserved, p 62; Robin Matthews © *Tatler*, p 64; John W Benson p 65 (bottom right); Fritz Von Der Schulenburg p 69; Peter Cook p 85; Claude Mercier pp 90-95, 97-101; Georgina Masson from *Italian Villas & Palaces*, published by Thames & Hudson, p 99 (bottom left); *Richmond & Twickenham Times* p 102; David Page of DP Photographic, London, pp 110, 111.

The publishers also acknowledge their indebtedness to the following books, which were consulted for reference or as sources of illustrations: Giovanantonio Rusconi – *Dell' Architettura*; Chambers – *Civil Architecture*; Lucy Archer – *Raymond Erith*; Palladio – *The Four Books of Architecture*; Rossi – *Studio D' Architettura Civile*; Galerie Antique, ou Collection des Chefs – D' Oeuvre D' Architecture.

Cover: Corinthian capitals for the doorcase at the Dower House, Little Roydon, Kent
P 2: Venetian Villa loggia, Regents Park

First published in Great Britain in 1993 by
ACADEMY EDITIONS
An imprint of the Academy Group Ltd
42 Leinster Gardens London W2 3AN
Published in Germany by
ERNST & SOHN
Hohenzollerndamm 170, D-1000, Berlin 31
members of the VCH PUBLISHING GROUP

ISBN 1-85490-146-X (HB)
ISBN 1-85490-147-8 (PB)

Distributed to the trade in the United States of America in 1993 by
ST MARTIN'S PRESS
175 Fifth Avenue New York NY 10010

Printed and bound in Singapore

CONTENTS

DRAWING OF GRIFFIN FOR DOWNING COLLEGE

INTRODUCTION

BY KENNETH POWELL

Quinlan Terry is at his most serious-minded, grave even, when he talks not about architecture but about the state of the world. The two are, of course, closely connected in his mind and he has spoken of their relationship on many occasions. Terry, for all the success of his practice, does not live for architecture and believes that the sort of architecture he practises is sometimes at odds with the modern world. For Terry, that is part of its attraction since he sees the modern world (like modern architecture) as fundamentally wrong-headed, heading towards disaster on all levels. He was schooled in the tradition of the Modern Movement, which saw architecture as a means of reforming society and improving the lot of man. This ideology he has rejected totally. Yet he would not perhaps dispute the judgement of that great Modernist teacher Siegfried Giedion, that architecture is the index to the character of an era. 'However much a period may try to disguise itself', wrote Giedion, 'its real nature will show through its architecture . . .' Precisely so, Terry responds. A mechanistic way of building divorced from nature and tradition, rooted in the extravagant use of materials and energy, and destined for rapid obsolescence, reflects a materialistic age which has lost sight of the things that really matter.

Above all, the 20th century has lost sight of God, the God who Terry believes is its Maker and Redeemer. The way to saving the world he insists, is not through architecture but through faith. He derives more satisfaction from studying the Bible and serving as a lay preacher than from designing buildings. 'Architecture', he says, 'is not a means of Grace', not a crusade. It is a business which, like any other, should be conducted honourably. As a Christian, Terry endorses the view of the 17th-century poet-priest George Herbert:

> Who sweeps a room, as for thy laws
> Makes that and the action fine.

But he practises architecture to feed his family, not to save his soul.

If Terry has sometimes been presented, to his dismay, as a latter-day Pugin (or worse still, Ruskin) promoting Christian architecture, he must himself bear some of the blame. In an often-quoted essay on the origins of the Orders published in 1983 (and reprinted here), he portrayed Classicism as having its origins in divine inspiration. More recently, he has instead stressed the essentially reasonable and practical aspects of Classical architecture. Both Pugin and Ruskin, he recalls, confused the objectives of art and religion – and ended their days insane . . .

Terry speaks disapprovingly of the 'Ruskinian heresy' of salvation through design – an error into which contemporary architects of more than one persuasion are tempted to fall. He finds his position as a symbol of traditionalism a little embarrassing, since he is certainly determined to avoid being bracketed as a member of any school or campaign, however worthy its aims. He has largely shunned the 'debate' about architecture launched by the Prince of Wales (a supporter of his work) in the mid-80s and is reluctant to criticise the work of individual architects. It is not easy to persuade Terry to visit London – he prefers to remain in Dedham and get on with his work.

Terry's determined independence of thought and disillusionment with modern architecture became apparent while he was a student, but was reinforced through his long association with Raymond Erith (1904-1973), whose practice he continues under the title Erith & Terry. Erith was tolerated by the architectural establishment (he became a Royal Academician and served on the Royal Fine Art Commission) because his lonely crusade for traditional architecture seemed doomed to failure. Confined largely to building one-off private houses, he could safely be tolerated. In contrast, the opprobrium heaped on Terry's work is the outcome of his advance into areas from which Erith had been successfully excluded.

Not every adverse critic of Terry's work is a hardline Modernist (indeed, the sheer integrity of his approach inspires respect from defenders of the Modernist tradition who find Post-Modernism facile and opportunist). Some allege that his buildings fail to take up the 'progressive' theme in Erith's work and if anything, reflect a drift backwards into the derivative and imitative. Terry's sometimes flamboyant use of ornament and contempt (as some see it) for the niceties of 'context' have further fuelled a campaign to discredit his achievement.

Terry faces the issue of imitation head on. Like Demetri Porphyrios, an architect whom he respects, he stresses that imitation has been a central feature of Western architecture for thousands of years. 'Negation of the past' is the essence of modern architecture: 'to ignore tradition is childish, but to do the opposite, like the Moderns, is . . . words fail me. I think it must be the product of a diseased mind!'

But, for a Classical architect working in late 20th-century Britain, which 'tradition' counts most – Vitruvius? Palladio? Chambers? Lutyens?

While Erith's work could not unreasonably be located at the end of a long line of traditional country builders (an interpretation of which he approved), Terry's taste is more exotic. His biographer, Clive Aslet, has called him a Mannerist. In particular he looks to Palladio and more controversially to Italian Mannerist and Baroque precedents. As early as 1967, when he spent the winter studying the architecture of Rome, he was interested in Classical buildings of all periods and was prepared to take an inclusive view of Classicism. (Even Gothic architecture, he concludes, is a variant of Classicism, if a rather perverse one.) Terry's respect for the work of the English Palladians is tempered, one suspects, with a degree of impatience with the restraint and (on occasion) thinness of their buildings. He is emphatically not a neo-Georgian. Nor does he like his Classicism elemental – only recently has he become interested in the pure Greek Doric Order, previously preferring it in its Palladian transmutation. (Greece, indeed, has never been a source of direct inspiration.) In recent works, like the Howard Building in Cambridge, the still continuing series of villas in Regents Park, London, and the designs for an office block at Paternoster Square, next to St Paul's, Terry has been prepared to use ornament lavishly and to vary his style in a way some deem arbitrary. (Soane, it might be recalled, commonly offered designs for buildings in more than one style, leaving the client to choose.)

Terry's exoticism stems from his sincere concern for beauty.

Lavishness and display, and picturesque effects, where appropriate, are, he believes, a modest rejoinder to the utilitarian ugliness of the modern world. However, he is concerned that ornament should be 'meaningful'. For example, that attached to the new library at Downing College has been carefully thought out in terms of the academic disciplines to be studied within its walls. Terry's religious fundamentalism and critical view of consumer society might lead one to think of him as a puritan, someone who wishes to suppress even the most harmless forms of pleasure. However, nothing could be further from the truth: he places delight high amongst the proper aims of architecture, and sees the architect's task as that of instilling beauty into what could be simply functional.

But for Terry, aesthetics are subordinate to deeper issues. Modern architecture is ugly, he says, but its ugliness (like that of modern painting and music) is, 'the expression of an age which is morally and spiritually bankrupt – a world that knows not what to do, nor where to turn'. It is also an illogical, wasteful way of building. Traditional buildings simply last longer and using traditional materials leads, Terry believes, inexorably to the creation of architecture. There is a streak of rationalism in his thinking which is more concerned with 'naturalness' and sound building than with the application of stylistic details.

To his own surprise perhaps, Quinlan Terry finds himself endorsing some contemporary trends in thought. 'I suppose the Green movement is on our side', he admits, conceding his own growing emphasis on the wastefulness and environmental pollution of much modern development.

However, he does not believe that an architect should refrain from building simply because the brief is not 100 percent to his liking; 'I do want to build', he says. At Richmond Riverside he had to compromise: first on materials, using reconstituted stone to reduce costs; and second, on the internal arrangement of the buildings, which is entirely modern. The choice was simple – adapt to the developer's needs or give up the job. Richmond was built and has become an icon of traditional urban design, of the revival of civil architecture. Terry's equally bold proposals for the centre of the Suffolk town of Bury St Edmunds seem destined to remain on paper, but their humane radicalism fosters criticisms of Terry's work as mere pastiche. For Downing College library, Terry has had to accept the logic of modern construction in the case of underground book stacks with one foot thick concrete walls, while steel trusses and purlins make sense for the roof. (Timber of the quality used by the Georgians is not available today and would cost far more.) In any case, the open plan of the building – a reflection of modern approaches to comfort and security – suggests the use of modern materials. 'If you decided to be a purist, it couldn't be built with the money available. Some problems, I concede, are best tackled in a modern way', he says. 'I don't, for example, go to work on a horse or write with a quill.' (But, he adds, perhaps he *should*

revert to older, more civilised ways of doing things . . .) If a client has the funds to commit, he should, Terry says, use the best materials – reconstituted stone is good but can never match the real thing in the long term. Local materials should be used wherever possible, because they tend to meet the specific needs of an area. But Terry has no moral dilemma over materials. Indeed, he never agonises over his jobs. If he accepts a commission, he does it to the best of his ability, believing that the first responsibility of an architect is to the client. There are not enough enlightened clients to change the face of Britain, but this 'remnant, their sights set on a better world' (here speaks Quinlan Terry, the crusader) can keep the flame of architecture burning in a hostile world. Does it matter if they are commercial developers, wealthy individuals wanting luxurious homes or garden follies, churchmen wanting more convenient and uplifting places to worship, or colleges wanting more space for books and lectures? It is not the architect's job to dictate to his client.

Although Quinlan Terry has been anxious, like Leon Krier, to dispel the idea that Classicism in architecture is the corollary of a conservative (or even fascist) political order, he would readily admit that architecture and ideology cannot be entirely divorced. Speaking at the Oxford Union a few years ago, he called on 'generations of Englishmen' as his witnesses to the superior wisdom of traditional building. The political context of his work is necessarily conservative – just as Modern architecture is associated in his view with 'a restless desire to break up the order of the world'. There is more than a hint in his utterances of the belief (voiced so prosaically by Reginald Blomfield in the 1930s) that Modern architecture is a foreign import England does not need. Yet Terry could scarcely be accused of insularity. If he is, then so were Inigo Jones and Robert Adam. Neither is his conservatism at all straightforward. Although his practice boomed in the Thatcher years with a growing list of 'establishment' clients, and despite his declaration to the effect that 'I do not build for the masses', he sincerely wants to change the way that people live. However, he does not believe that 'social engineering' works. A better society can only be achieved through the individual regeneration – big business is as much the enemy as the state, the 'progress' represented by mass production and technological advance a dangerous delusion. (Progress, Terry argues, can only come through faith . . .)

Placed by Robert Stern amongst the so-called 'canonic' Classicists, for whom the observance of rules matters more than the freedom to invent, Quinlan Terry might appear to be a peculiarly English figure, a nonconformist, even an eccentric, and a vital element in the pluralistic British scene. This image devalues his achievements. He builds with care, with commitment, with love, and rejects the commonplace and the conventional. His work, although he would detest the description, is, in its own modest way, revolutionary.

I
PRIMVS
LIBER
~
SKETCHES
&
MEASURED
DRAWINGS

MCMXCII
AD

EXTRACT FROM ROMAN SKETCHBOOK, 1968

I came to Rome to learn mainly by measuring. On comparing my measurements with those of the masters I found not only that mine differed from theirs, but that theirs differed from each other. Moreover, the architects who had gone before me had given their measured drawings the stamp of their own style and period. Palladio gave something of his own character to the buildings of ancient Rome. Desgodetz in turn would give Palladio's version of the Roman Orders something of his authoritarian, academic, outlook. In the early 19th century Taylor and Cressy went back to the originals, measuring with great care – only to give their drawings something of the Victorian spirit which was to follow. Classical architecture is in fact a principle which is subject to changes in style. Style can be imposed on it and can change its character, so much so that one can tell the period and nationality even in a measured drawing of an old building. What interested me about this is that while Classical architecture is a principle, its style evolves. Its strength is that it can adapt itself to change without sacrificing its principle.

I am continually asked this question: what is the relevance of Classical architecture to the present day? The simple answer is that as things stand at present there is none. The modern world has rejected Classical architecture. It has rejected all past styles. What is more, it has rejected the principles on which all architecture in the past depended. Modern architecture, ie the style internationally adopted at the present time, is in fact revolutionary. It is not constructive. Its object is to do the opposite of what was done in the past and it is content to leave it at that. It is true that it depends on the past, in the sense that the negation of the past is its *raison d'être*, but apart from that it has no driving force.

I would therefore be the first to admit that Classical architecture has no relevance to the present day. But I question whether an architecture which is based on the negation of the past can survive. Something more constructive is bound to follow – and in that case Classical architecture, which more completely than any other embodies the principles of architecture, is relevant. It will of course be said that Modern architecture was a necessary reaction to a decadent tradition. I would agree. But my position now is that of a critic of the critics. My view is that Modern architecture is a failure. It has no life. It could not evolve a new architecture because it had no new principle to replace the one which it set out to destroy. It was stillborn.

I find in Classical architecture everything that is lacking in Modern architecture:

Classical architecture is functional, which Modern architecture in spite of its aspirations is not.

Classical architecture is based on using materials and methods of construction in such a way that they provide a durable and dependable building. No Modern building will last. Even Modern buildings of a temporary nature have an unnecessarily high maintenance cost.

Classical architecture is orderly where Modern is chaotic. It expresses its use and its construction. One can tell at a glance if a classic building is a church, a town hall or a house. Modern buildings are confused and express nothing except with the aid of lettering and symbols.

Classical architecture is dignified; it is capable of magnificence as well as humility. It can, by the use of its mouldings and vocabulary, express an infinite variety of moods and conditions of man whether it be national, social or historical. It is the expression of civilised man where every person is different. Modern architecture expresses revolutionary man where man is merely a unit.

Classical architecture is based on nature, on the forms and proportions commonly found in creation and music. The Modern, while giving lip-service to the 'modulor', is governed by nothing but an unnatural and inhuman standardisation imposed by machinery and technology.

Classical architecture is beautiful, Modern is ugly. (That this is generally accepted is demonstrated in any description of unspoilt country: unspoilt does not mean country without buildings; it means country without *modern* buildings.) It is the manifest intention of the Classical architect to achieve beauty. This is recognised in contemporary accounts where the emphasis is put on the just disposition of the parts to the whole, balance, harmony, grace etc. It is the manifest intention of Modern architects to achieve ugliness and brutality and to shock.

Classical architecture depends on function, durability, order, humanity, nature, and beauty. Modern architecture has none of these things.

I do not expect these views will convince a Modernist. Modernism is an emotional conviction which will not succumb to evidence or argument. It is a restless desire to do the opposite of what is right and good and harmonious; to break up the order of the world and upset the apple cart of accumulated knowledge and experience. It is not, as it boasts, a new thing; it is as old as mankind and has been seen at various times in the history of the world, but only recently has it had the facility to show itself in all its horror through architecture. People are at last beginning to vent their dissatisfaction with the whole Modern approach and to regard established Modern architecture as inadequate. The young are frustrated by it and many others are left with a feeling of helplessness, chiefly because they cannot see anything to replace it. Is it not now time to discard the Modern approach root and branch and return to the letter and spirit of the classic world?

> The thing that hath been, it is that which shall be; and that which is done is that which shall be done: and there is no new thing under the sun. Is there anything whereof it may be said, see, this is new? It hath been already of old time which was before us. (*Ecclesiastes*, Chapter 1, verses 9-10)

'Postscript of Roman Sketchbook, 1968', was translated into German and published in 1981 as part of In Opposition zur Moderne. Aktuelle Positionen in der Architektur.

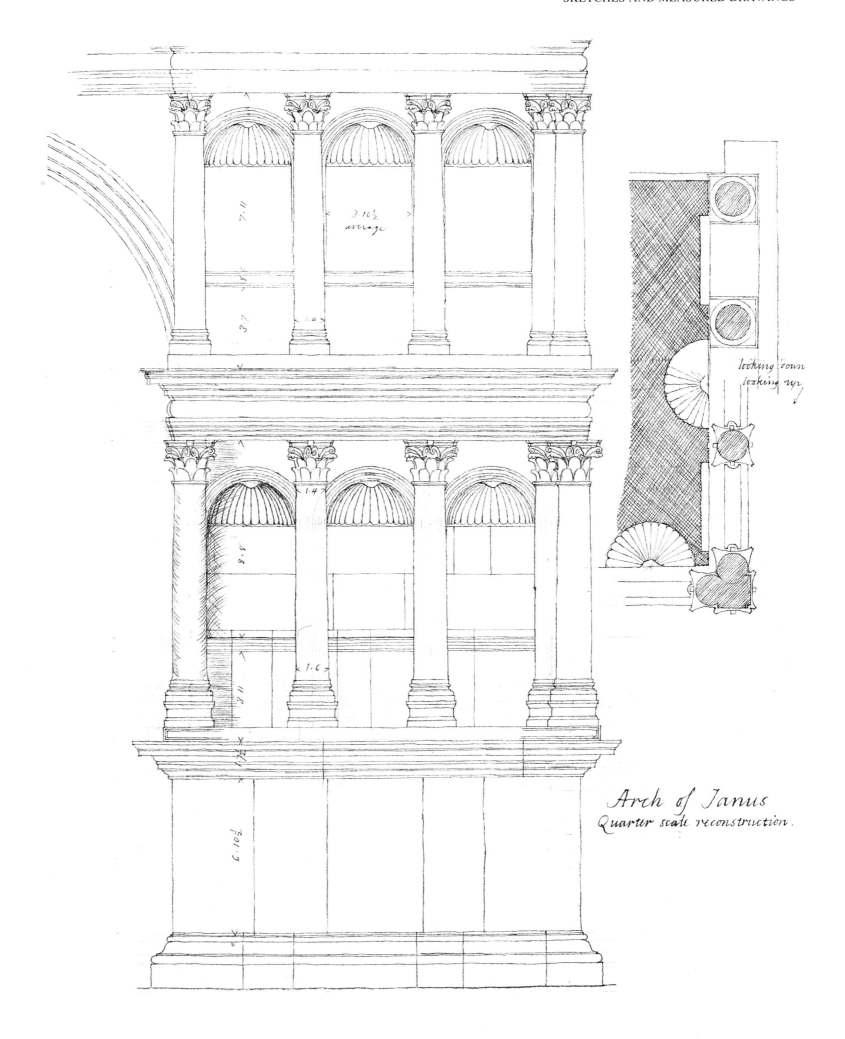

3·10½
average

7·11

3·7

1·4

looking down
looking up

8·5

1·4

1·6

3·11

6·10½

Arch of Janus
Quarter scale reconstruction.

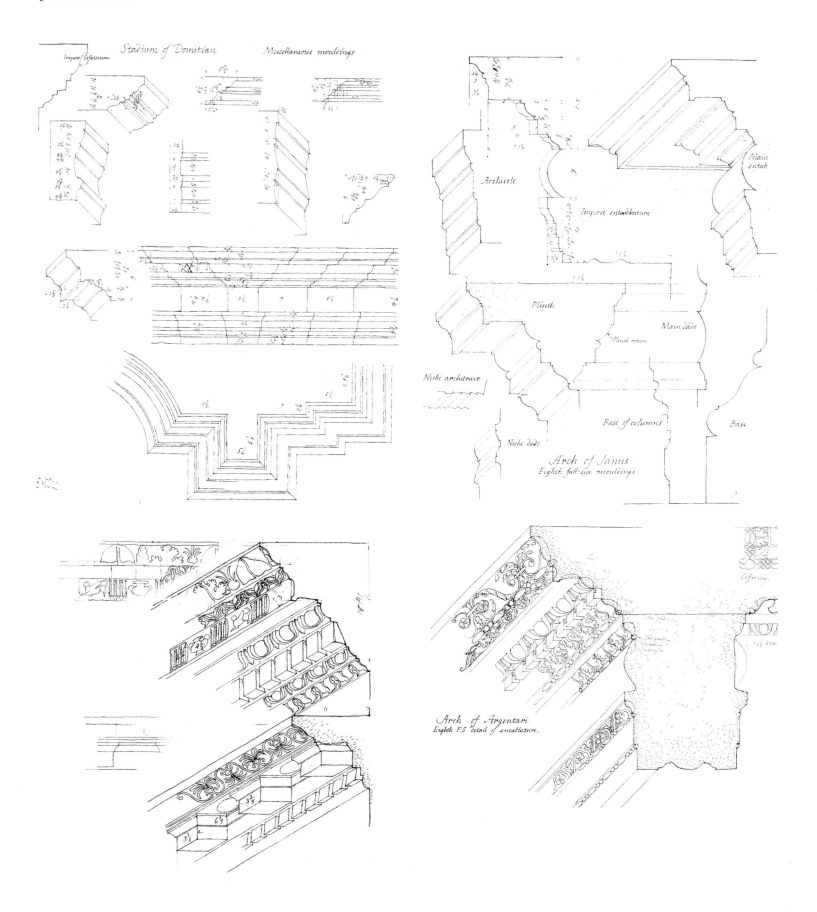

Stadium of Domitian

Miscellaneous mouldings

Arch of Janus
Eighth full-size mouldings

Arch of Argentari
Eighth F.S. detail of entablature.

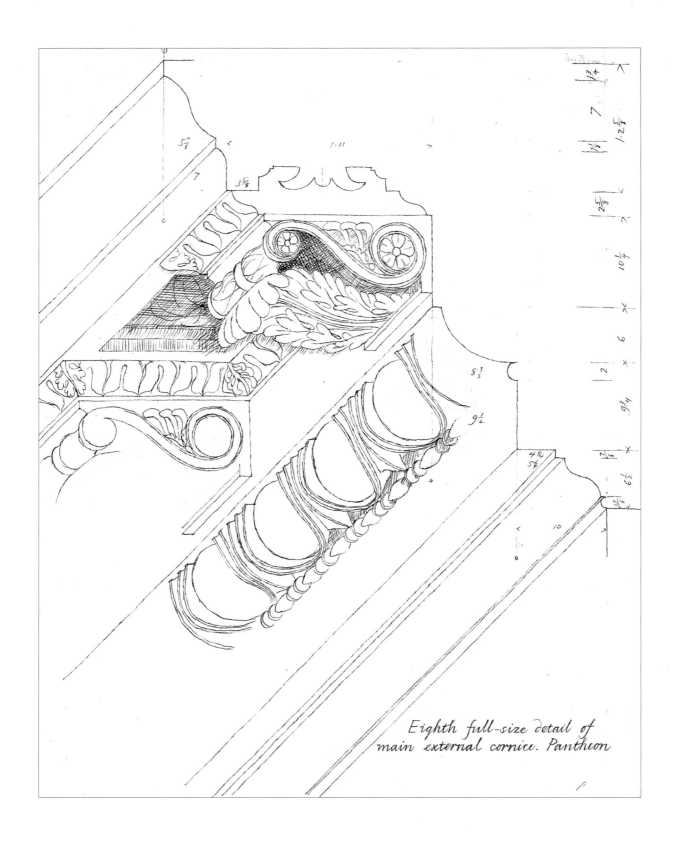

*Eighth full-size detail of
main external cornice. Pantheon*

ROMAN MOULDINGS

Roman mouldings, having developed on a greater scale and over a longer period than those of any other age before or since, have more variations and subtleties than Renaissance mouldings. They also have all the qualities that were picked up in subsequent Baroque periods: the use of breaks and sloping plates in the Stadium of Domitian; the almost Palladian orthodoxy of the Arch of Janus; the provocative errors in placing triglyphs on the face of the corona and modillions below the top cyma in the Vatican Museum; the deeply drilled enrichments of every moulding in the Arch of Argentari; and the sheer scale of the Pantheon, all demonstrate the inexhaustible and lively variations available which later ages have rediscovered and made their own.

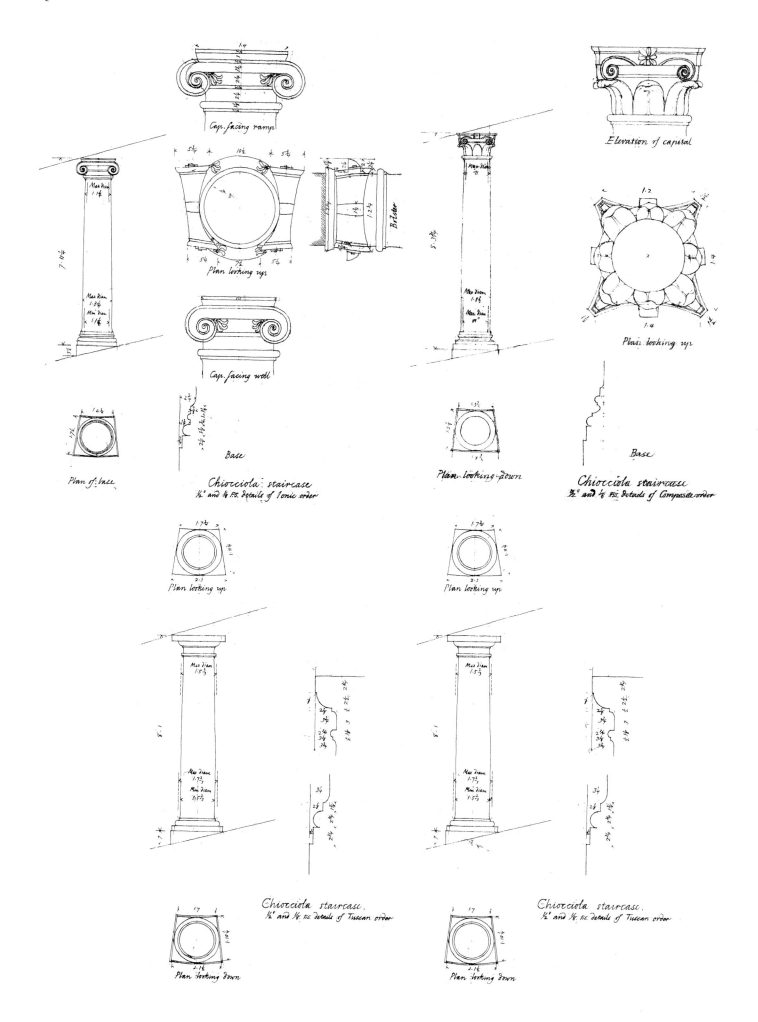

Cap. facing ramp

Plan looking up

Bolster

Cap. facing wall

Plan of base

Base

Chiocciola staircase
½" and ⅛ F.S. details of Ionic order

Plan looking up

Elevation of capital

Plan looking up

Plan looking down

Base

Chiocciola staircase
½" and ⅛ F.S. details of Composite order

Plan looking up

Chiocciola staircase.
½" and ⅛ F.S. details of Tuscan order

Plan looking down

Chiocciola staircase.
½" and ⅛ F.S. details of Tuscan order

Plan looking down

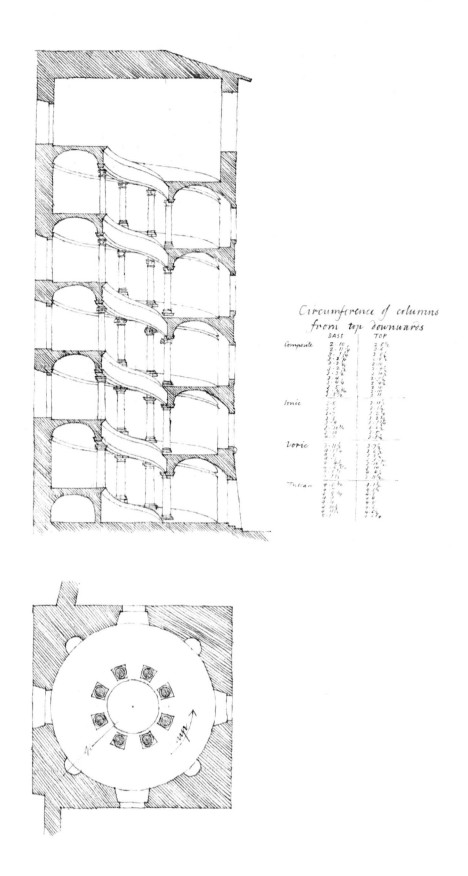

Circumference of columns
from top downwards

CHIOCCIOLA STAIRCASE, VATICAN

From these measurements it is evident that each column is progressively smaller as the staircase ascends and that the size of each bottom diameter is the same as the top diameter of the column below it. The very pure use *of number in this staircase is typical of the work of Bramante. Letarouilly's measurements fail to pick up these subtleties by only measuring one example of each Order and presuming the others to be the same.*

0   5   10   15   20

Mens et delt. Quinlan Terry 1968

S. Maria in Campitelli, Rome
Sixteenth scale elevation of facade
Designed by Carlo Rainaldi, circa: 1666

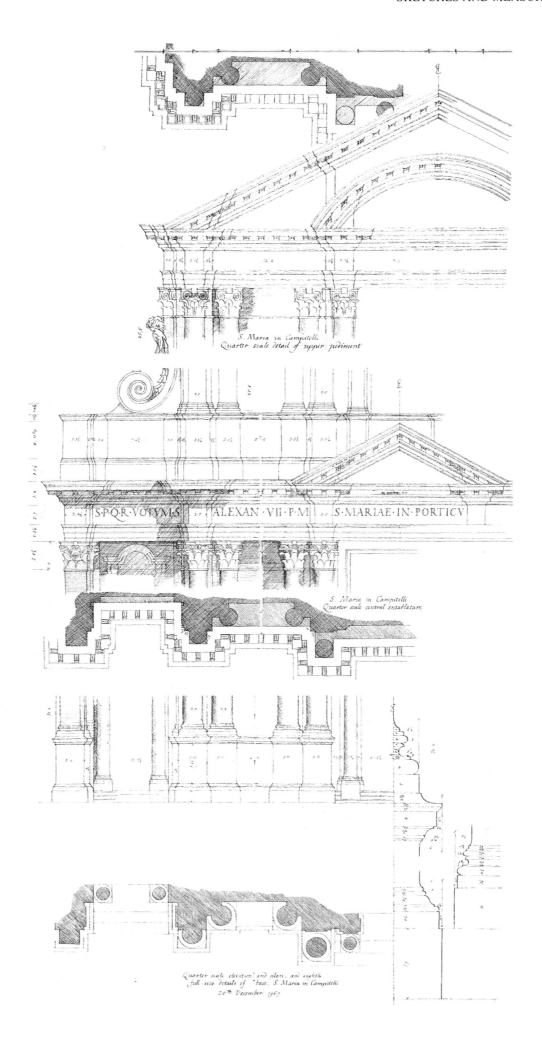

S. Maria in Campitelli.
Quarter scale detail of upper pediment

S·P·Q·R·VOTVMS   ALEXAN·VII·P·M   S·MARIAE·IN·PORTICV

S. Maria in Campitelli
Quarter scale central entablature.

Quarter scale elevation and plan, and eighth
full size details of base. S. Maria in Campitelli
20ᵗʰ December 1967

17

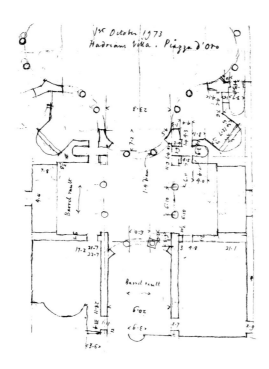

1st October 1973
Hadrian's Villa. Piazza d'Oro

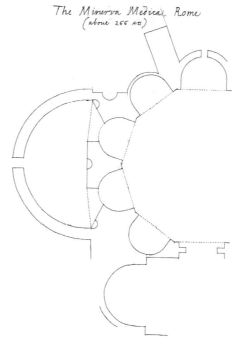

The Minerva Medica, Rome
(about 266 AD)

Scale 1/250

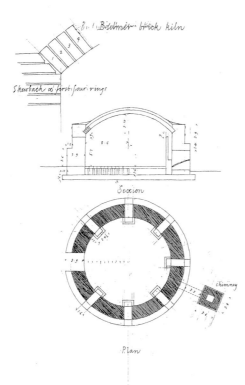

Brickmaker's brick kiln

Section

Plan

Eighth scale.

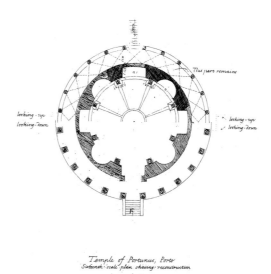

Temple of Portunus, Porto
Sixteenth scale plan showing reconstruction.

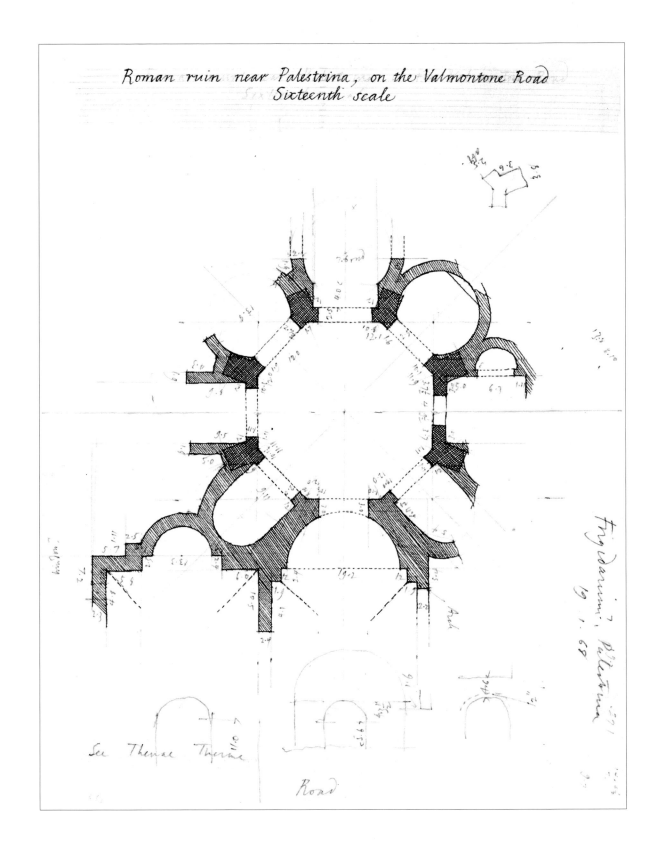

Roman ruin near Palestrina, on the Valmontone Road
Sixteenth scale

DOMES

These drawings are a small part of a 1972 study on unreinforced dome construction in Italy and the Middle East. The small brick kiln, only 17 feet in diameter, was constructed without the use of shuttering, by laying the brick skewback in sticky mortar on a slope, so that when one ring has been completed it acts as a wedge in an arch and cannot therefore fall in. Choisy said that it is as easy to build a dome as it is difficult to build a barrel vault. All Roman and Islamic domes were constructed on this principle without using shuttering.

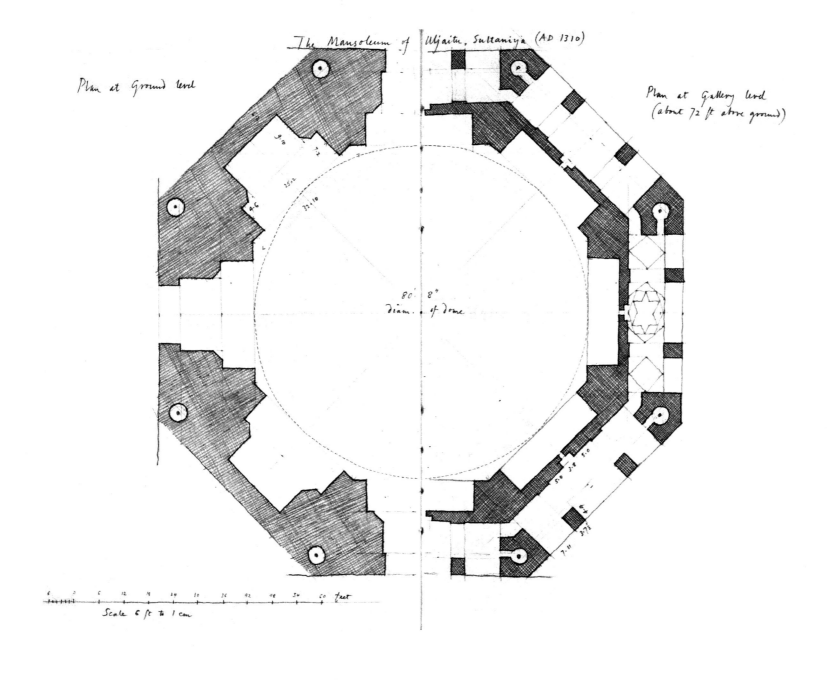

The Mausoleum of Uljaitu, Sultaniya (AD 1310)

Plan at Ground level

Plan at Gallery level
(about 72 ft above ground)

80' 8"
diam. of dome

Scale 6 ft to 1 cm

Mausoleum of Uljaitu, Sultanijeh.

On Friday 13th April 1973 Erich & I were lucky enough to be taken to see this building. I say lucky because not only was it entirely scaffolded which allowed us to measure the section but also because Friday is the Moslem rest day which meant that the over-jealous Italian supervisor who is determined to stop anyone gaining material for publication was having his day off. We had two hours on the job. Erich measured the plan, I did the section.

I think this egg-shaped dome is a structural necessity brought about by two things; the need to keep the whole of the structure in compression & also the need to construct the dome without centering. The shortage of timber forced the builders to design their domes to be self-supporting during construction so that there was probably no more than a small amount of local propping off a timber scaffolding. A closer inspection of the dome bears this out. (see diagram)

At a point about half way up the dome there was a portion opened up for repair where I was able to see the construction. The bricks (or tiles) are 2 ins thick & generally 10 ins square but there are many half-tiles 10" x 5". They are

laid with a thick mortar joint almost horizontally with a very slight tilt towards the centre. The inner skin is two tiles thick, the outer skin is one tile thick so the space in the middle at the position I was measuring was 2 ft 2 ins across & 4 ft between two vertical ribs 1 ft 6 ins thick. There were two rows of horizontal bracing in this space between the ribs in the height of the dome. I think there are sixteen ribs on the circumference.

* Raymond Erich RA. Died November same year.

Section through centre of typical bay

Scale 6 ft to 1 cm approx
(measured off scaffolding)

8 squinches per bay

3 squinches form transition

Minaret

Gallery.

Some bays have semi domes

horizontal rotating line

3.6 diam

25.2

32.10

40'.4"

(43'.4" into corners of octagon)

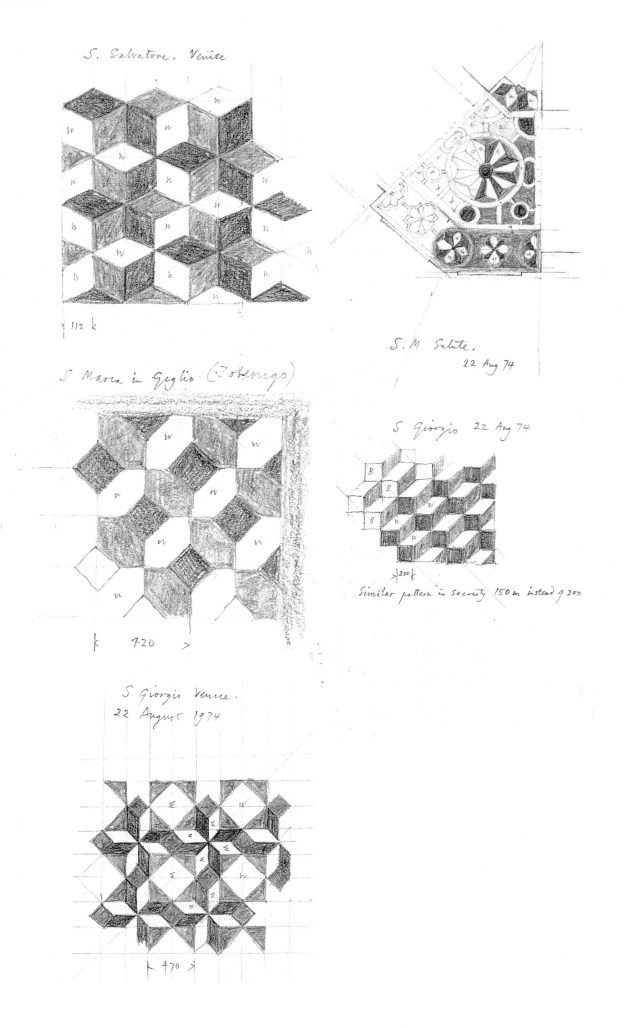

S. Salvatore. Venice

112

S. M. Salute.
22 Aug 74

S Maria in Giglio (Zobenigo)

420

S Giorgio 22 Aug 74

200

Similar pattern in Sacristy 150 m instead of 200

S Giorgio Venice.
22 August 1974

470

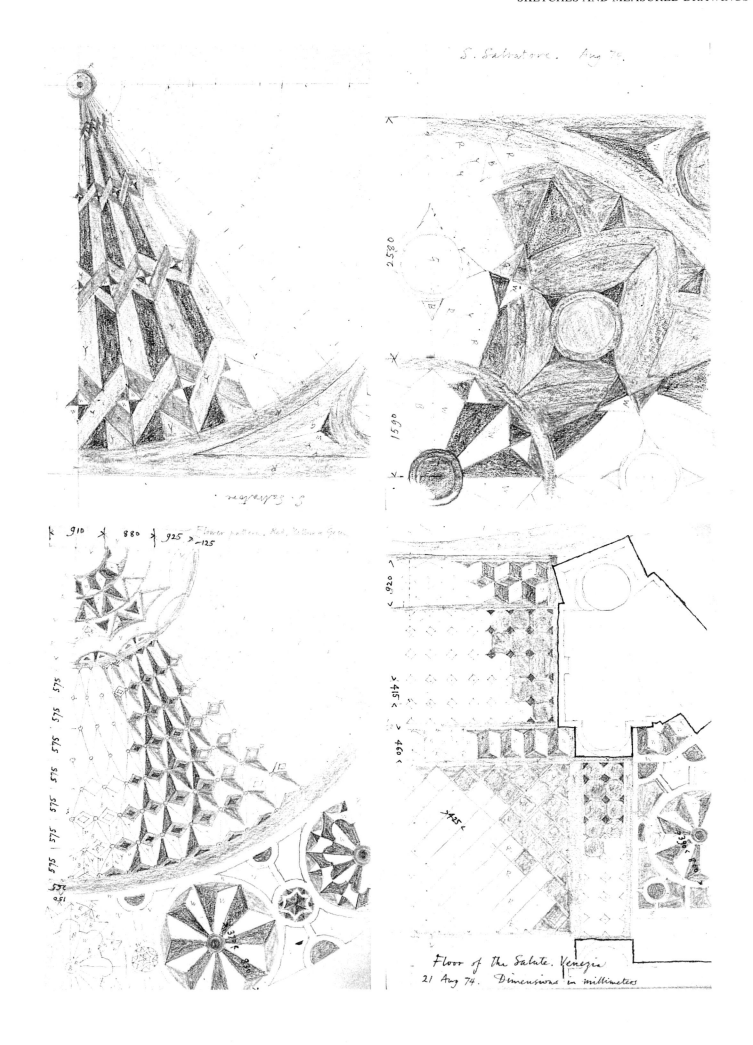

S. Salvatore. Aug 74.

Floor of the Salute. Venezia
21 Aug 74. Dimensions in millimeters

Chiesa Della Maddalena. Front by Giuseppe Sardi
Rome.
1735

Loreto
31 August 1982

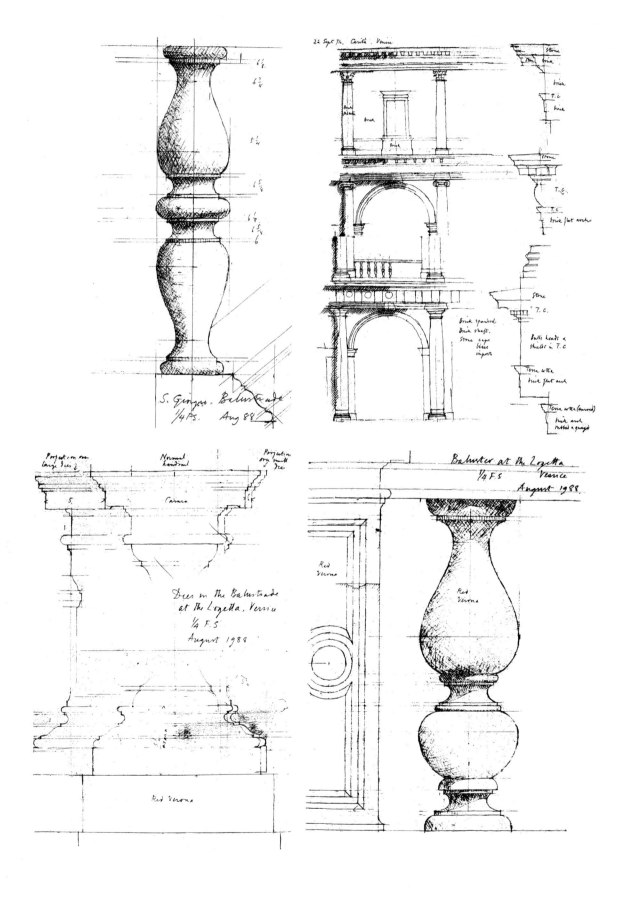

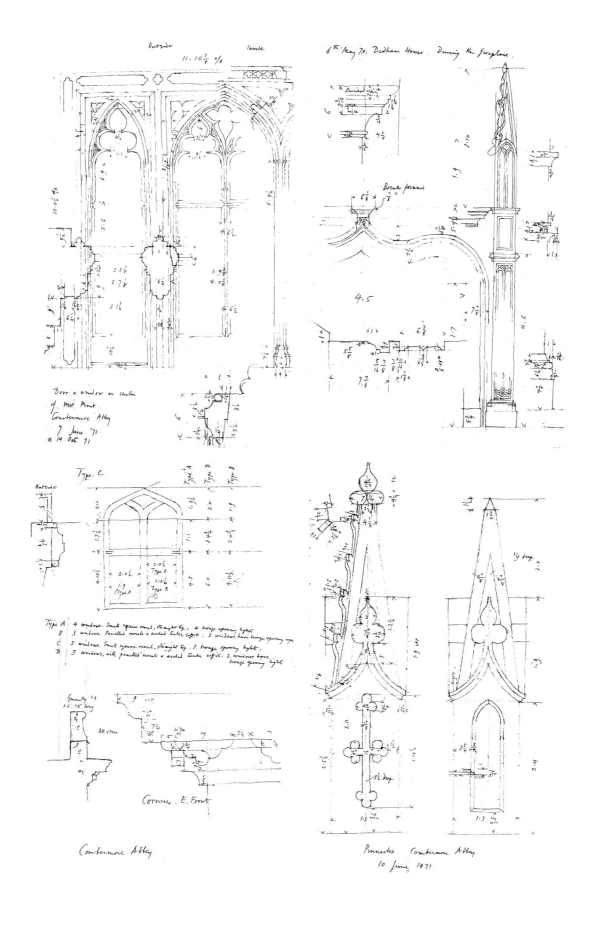

Comtermore Abbey

Pinnacles Comtermore Abbey
10 June 1971

Anna ½ inch scale
30 April 72

Anna 25 July 1973

		Quinlan		Christine		Lizzie at 8		Anna at 6 1/2		Francis at 3		Approx ppn.
Overal height	A	6.2 7/8		5.3 3/8		4.3 1/2		3.11		3.2		
Span of arms	B	6.5 1/2		5.1 1/2		4.2		3.5 1/2		3.1		A : B
Shoulders	C	1.6		1.3		1.0		11 1/4		9		
Hips. Width	D	1.3		1.1		9 1/2		8 1/8				
depth	E	8 1/2		8 1/4		5 1/2		5				
Hips to floor	F	3.9	1/1.6	3.2	1/1.6	2.8		2.3		1.9		F : A
Knee to floor	G	2.0	1/1.8	1.6	1/2.1	1.4		1.2		10 1/2		G : F
Belly button to floor	H	3.9		3.1		2.6 1/8		2.2 3/4				
Finger to shoulder	I	2.9		2.3		1.10		1.8				
Finger to elbow	J	1.7 3/4		1.4 1/2		1.1		1.0				
Hand. Length	K	8		6 3/4		5 5/8		5		4 1/4		
width	L	3 1/2		3 1/8		2 3/4		2 5/8		2		
Foot. Length	M	11 1/4		9		8 1/4		6 3/4		6		
width	N	4		3 1/2		3 1/8		2 3/4				
First digit of thumb	O	1 1/2		1 1/4		1 1/4		1		7/8		
Head. Height	P	8 3/4	1/8.5	7 7/8	1/8.2	7 3/4	1/6.6	7 5/8	1/6.1	7 1/4	1/5.2	P : A
width	Q	5 1/2		5		4 7/8		4 1/4		4 1/2		
depth	R	8 1/4		6 7/8		7 3/8		6 1/2	1/1.1	7 1/4	1/1	R : P
Chin to eye	S	4 5/8		3 3/4		3 5/8		3 1/2		3 1/8		
to nose	T	2 5/8		2 1/8		2 1/4		2 1/8		1 7/8		
to mouth	U	1 7/8		1 1/2		1 1/2		1 3/8		1 1/4		
Chin to hair	V	8	1/1	6 3/4	1/1	6 1/4	1/1.1	5 5/8	1/1.1	5 3/4		K : V
Eye width	W	1 3/8		1 1/4		1 1/8		1 1/8		1		
space between	X	1 1/8		1 5/16		1		1 1/16		1		
Crutch to floor	Y	3.1		2.6 1/4								
Span	Z	9										

'Therefore, since nature has designed the human body so that its members are duly proportional to the frame as a whole, it appears that the ancients had good reason for their rule, that in perfect building the different members must be in exact symmetrical relations to the general scheme.' (Vitruvius, Book 3, Chapter 1.)

The above measurements of the Terry family test the validity of Vitruvius's statement.

II

SECVNDVS

LIBER

~

SMALL

BUILDINGS

MCMXCII
AD

A QUESTION OF STYLE

I feel that 'the question of style' is so bound up with an attitude to construction and materials that it cannot be considered on its own. Let me illustrate this with a most elementary example, of a brick garden wall.

I often pass an old wall built along a slope which looks something like the illustration below left. It is nine inches thick, Flemish bond in lime mortar with the brick courses running parallel with the slope. It is about a quarter of a mile long.

On the other side of the road there is the modern solution to the same problem, which looks like the other illustration, below right. A nine inch brick wall with the courses level built in cement mortar and therefore needing expansion joints every 30 feet, as well as a needless damp course of bitumen above ground and under the coping. The expansion joints have filled with grit and pebbles so that the wall can no longer expand, with the result that cracks have now appeared between the designed joints. The damp course has weakened the wall at the point where it ought to be strongest and one section has blown over.

Even this simple example gives abundant illustration of what happens when the experience of tradition is unwisely cast aside and what direct effect such a change of attitude has on the appearance, or if you like the style, of any structure.

Classical architecture, like the old wall in my example, is accumulated knowledge and experience; where the style evolves and the principles based on common sense remain. On the other hand, Modernism is not like the new wall based upon accepted laws of common-sense building. It is therefore a fashion rather than a style because it has no underlying principles, except possibly to do the opposite of what was done before.

If you allow yourself to design within the constraints imposed by common-sense traditional building you will very soon find yourself working in the Classical vein. And if you are not frightened of the consequences (or the criticism of the Modernists), you will very soon begin to discover the wisdom of the five Orders.

I am not afraid of the criticism or the consequences; I would go further. I enjoy what I do enormously, it gives me pleasure. It is like a three-dimensional game of chess where the rules (or the gambits) can lead to endless possibilities; some very simple and obvious and others rather more sophisticated.

Taken from a lecture given at the RIBA on 21 November 1978. Published by Architectural Design, *volume 49, no 3/4, in 1979, and subsequently in Dutch in* Panorama van de avant-garde.

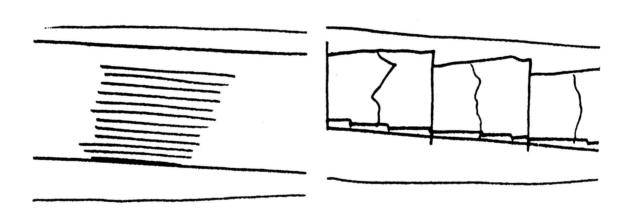

MISS **WATT'S** NEW CROQUET SHED, AYNHO

MISS WATT'S NEW CROQUET SHED, AYNHO

PRIMITIVE HUT
WEST GREEN, HAMPSHIRE, 1975

The Vitruvian idea of the Doric hut has often been used by theorists to give authenticity to Classical ornament. This is achieved by showing the practical origins of Doric detail and thus demonstrating the inevitability of *their forms. The Doric hut at West Green expounds these ideas through the use of shafts, capitals, architraves, triglyphs and a pediment, all of which are used as purely constructional elements.*

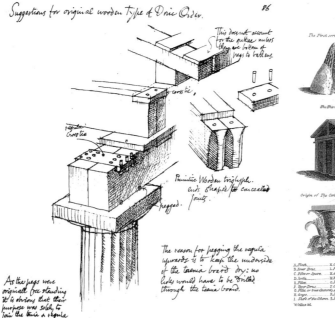

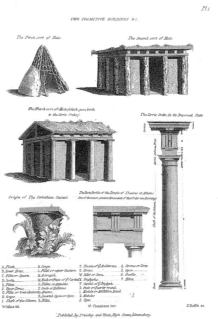

EYDON HALL COTTAGE
EYDON, NORTHAMPTONSHIRE, 1989-91

This small cottage has a total area of just over 1,000 square feet. It was built in 1990, in natural Hornton stone with stone-mullioned windows and leaded lights.

It continues the tradition which has been used in Eydon High Street since the Middle Ages, with the intention that those who see it will think it has always been there.

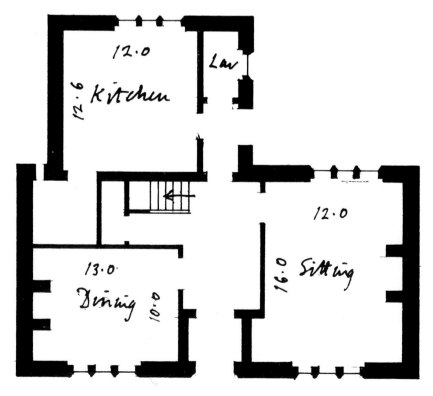

THE HERMITAGE
CRICHEL, DORSET, 1983-86

The building, a simple bungalow designed for a retired bachelor, is built in the Dorset vernacular of brick and flint in bands with stone quoins, and a thatched roof.

The bungalow has a T-shaped plan, and is organised around a central elliptical hall; eight doors lead off from the hall to all of the rooms.

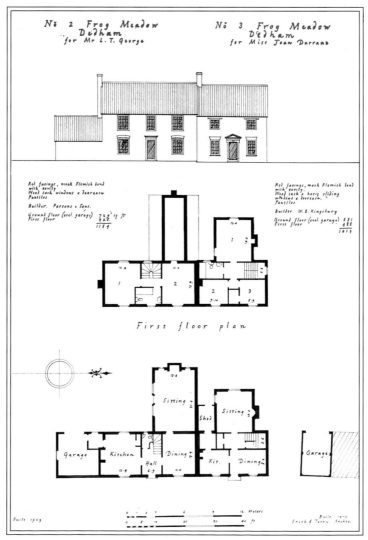

Nº 2 Frog Meadow
Dedham
for Mr L. T. George

Nº 3 Frog Meadow
Dedham
for Miss Joan Durrant

First floor plan

FROG MEADOW
DEDHAM, ESSEX, 1967-80

A row of seven houses in Dedham High Street. The first three were built before Raymond Erith's death in 1973, with the remaining four completed by 1980. The houses demonstrate many of the variations of the North Essex vernacular: the roofs are of plain tile, pantile and slate, and the walls are of brick and stucco; there are casements and sash windows, and the Orders employed are Doric and Ionic.

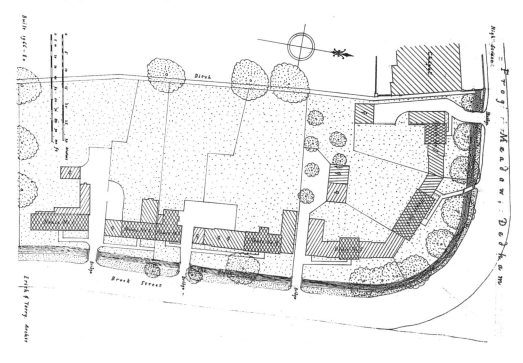

FARNBOROUGH DOWNS FARM AND COTTAGE
BERKSHIRE, 1984-89

Built in the Berkshire Downs, this modest-sized country house is attached to existing buildings on the west and forms the focal point of a number of farm buildings. It is built in local red-multi brickwork and stone dressings, with a steep plain tile roof. The centrepiece has a superimposed Tuscan and Ionic Order, with a simple bold modillion cornice, pediment and finials. The cornice is taken around the eaves of the main two-storey part of the building, which allows sufficient scale for a central hall and a large room on either side on the ground and first floors. The accommodation is extended within the roof space to provide additional bedrooms should the need arise.

The three-bedroom cottage on the same farm has a superficial area of about 1,000 square feet. It was built for the use of one of the farm workers, and stands in an important position in relation to the rest of the farm. The external walls are of normal cavity construction, using snapped headers to achieve a Flemish bond in a local red-multi facing brick.

SALUTE BIRDCAGE, 1980

A birdcage in stainless steel wire and limewood, as based directly on S Maria della Salute, Venice. The proportions of all the Orders have been maintained but the mouldings have been simplified in order to make a new form and scale which is quite unlike any architectural model of the original.

S. Maria della Salute
Venice 8 September 1982

TEMPLE OF VENUS
WEST WYCOMBE, BUCKINGHAMSHIRE, 1981

The design for this building is based on an 18th-century sketch of a temple which may once have stood on the site. The design was developed into an elliptical plan, featuring 12 columns and a flint grotto at the base of a mound made of earth. The ellipsoidal plain tile roof is capped with a sphere and bold gadrooned ovolo moulding, which features are reminiscent of the garden buildings to be found at Stowe.

SUMMERHOUSE
THENFORD, NORTHAMPTONSHIRE, 1980-82

This small summerhouse is a Baroque essay in Clipsham and Hornton stone, employing half-engaged and fluted Corinthian and Composite pilasters with square and circular gadrooned finials and smooth and rusticated walling. The use of numbers governs the design, with the intercolumniation being three at the ends, four at the sides and five in the middle. All proportions relate to the bottom diameter in whole imperial numbers.

IVSTITIA ET IVDICIVM CORRECTIO

NYMPHAEUM
WEST GREEN, HAMPSHIRE, 1980

This eye-catcher is a flat brick wall with stucco and stone decorations, and has been set out according to the laws of parallel perspective with a vanishing point at eye level to a design of a fountain with a deeply curved back and niches. The shadows have been cast according to the normal laws of sciagraphy and painted on the wall. It was based on a similar trompe l' oeil nymphaeum in the Villa Garibaldi, Rome. Opposite is a view of Higham Hall, where the same principles and themes were applied in the form of a wall-painting.*

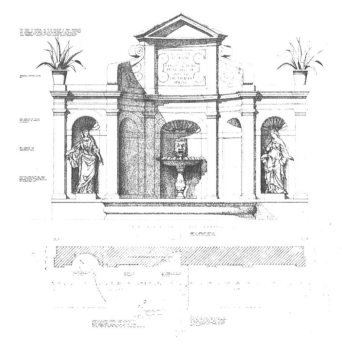

Tower of the Winds
OR
THE NEW VENTILATION SHAFT TERMINAL
FOR THE
VICTORIA LINE
AT
Gibson Square

III

TERTIVS

LIBER

~

VILLAS

&

COUNTRY

HOUSES

MCMXCII
AD

KINGSWALDEN NOTES

Classical architecture has been virtually dead for 200 years. Its remnants are now being throttled as the age of unenlightenment gains control. A detailed record of how it is done must be made in the hope that one day things may look up.

May 5th 1969

The house will stand where I believe four previous houses have stood, situated near the bottom of a valley with a good view to the south and an approach road from the north which skirts around an old elm avenue and terminates at the front door. The plan is self-evident: a hall and portico in the middle with a drawing room and sitting room on the west, balanced by a kitchen and dining room on the east. In between the hall and these reception rooms are smaller rooms; namely a staircase and flower room on one side, balanced by an office and gentlemen's cloakroom on the other. There is also a service wing to the east built around a yard or atrium comprising the pantry, nursery, staff rooms and garages with a butler's flat above.

Designing anything is a lengthy business with us. No genius stuff here of the maestro rushing it off with breathtaking originality in the heat of the moment. It's always one long concentrated effort which one has to attend to without distraction and error and even then there is a chance of it being a failure.

We always talk – endlessly – and then draw out the conclusions. We are usually dissatisfied with the result so we go on talking around the problem, mainly about common-sense construction and historical precedent. At this point a good deal of book searching takes place, including cribbing from sketchbooks, and walks are taken down the High Street to see how it should be done. Eventually, by a combination of discussion and drawing, a solution is arrived at.

Such is the case with the sash windows. The glazing bar is early – Queen Anne – and yet the house is really 1620 which is pre-sash window. The cill is from the Village Grammar School (about 1740). It looks like a Dutch sash where the box is solid with a groove cut out for the weights and yet the construction is English. The outer lining is very thick and really gives more the impression of an architrave than a sash box. These apparent contradictions might shock some historians, yet traditional architects have always felt free to take a leaf out of anybody's book to suit the needs of their times.

The dimensions of the Doric Order are given in English and Venetian and (where it is significant) in parts related to the bottom diameter.

The bases, imposts, caps, architraves and cornices are in worked Portland stone. The shafts are made up of two-inch thick stone discs built in to course with the brickwork. It is then plastered. The architraves on the south side span from column to column in one stone. On the north, the centre of the architrave is built into the brickwork as a keystone in reverse, thus halving the span between the columns.

Architecturally it is pretty pure Palladio. We imagine we have been into the master in Vicenza and are now, like Inigo Jones, trying to spread the good news with the aid of the *Quattro Libri* and very little else besides common-sense English building practice of the period; this, incidentally, is a key to the brickwork. But to return to the *Quattro Libri*: one can see the similarities with his Doric Order. We have only wavered for reasons of necessity, not originality; which are of course excusable. They are as follows:

1) Vignola's base being shorter helps to counteract the shortness of the shaft.
2) A cruder impost is used to help it look more countrified and because we wanted to use the Doric impost upstairs.

In the first book of the *Quattro Libri*, there are four entablatures which Palladio considers suitable for doors and windows. They are drawn with characteristic emphasis on the relation of the parts to the whole. They are unusually subtle and pleasing to the eye. We have used the first two of these for the principle doors on the ground floor: Palladio's first entablature for the doors in the portico – because their scale is a little bolder and more suitable externally – and the second entablature for the principle doors inside the building.

Architecturally these doors set the pace for much of the design later.

They have been designed to accord with the differences in the mouldings. There is no doorcase on the inside, just a simple architrave of reduced width which misses out the dado rail. One might expect this more in Italy than in England. The architect obviously had a taste for the continental. It is also more Baroque, but more about that later.

By strictly orthodox proportional standards, the column of the Ionic Order is short, the entablature is large, the cornice is very large. Alberti says:

> . . . the most expert artists among the ancients were of the opinion that an edifice was like an animal, so that in the formation of it we ought to imitate nature.

He then gives an example to illustrate the difference in the parts or members of beautiful things:

> . . . Some admire a woman for being extremely slender and fine shaped; the young gentleman in Terence preferred a girl that was plump and fleshy: you perhaps are for a medium between these two extremes, and would neither have her so thin as to seem wasted with sickness nor so strong and robust as if she were a ploughman in disguise and were fit for boxing: in short, you would have her such a beauty as might be formed by taking from the first what the second might spare. But then because one of these pleases you more than the other, would you therefore affirm the other to be not at all handsome? By no means; but there may be some hidden cause why one should please you more than the other . . .

I'm afraid we have not kept quite so close to the book as we did for the Doric. Necessity or expediency seem to have led us away a little. The column is 9' 18^1/$_8$" which is short: 9 x bottom diameter = 10' 6"; this column is nearer 8^1/$_2$ x bottom diameter.

May 1st 1970

As I go about this Sodom; as I read my newspaper and my Bible and see the vileness of man coupled with the 'advances' in destructive weapons; I come to the sad but unavoidable conclusion that sooner or later mankind will destroy itself:

The day of the Lord shall come as a thief in the night; in the which the heavens shall pass away with a great noise and the elements shall melt with fervent heat, the earth and the works that are therein shall be burned up. (*II Peter*, Chapter 3, verse 10)

All this makes me wonder why I spend my evenings scribbling in this book, when such knowhow will soon be of little use. Classical architecture is after all a tradition which has survived and been revived in a natural and stable world for thousands of years. The world is now no longer natural or stable. In this chaotic state it cannot last long.

Why then do I go on scribbling? It stops me going mad and such work is in itself satisfying. It is good at such a time to occupy one's mind with a timeless tradition and with beauty.

An enlightened soul might object: 'But aren't you a Christian? Should you not be going out and warning not only yourself but others of the wrath to come and proclaiming the fullness of the Gospel of Christ?' Answer: I do, when the spirit moves me, but to do that work properly one must be called. Until the call comes, I am wiser to stick to architecture. All work is holy.

So far I have been negative. I shall now be positive. We must look beyond our impending destruction to a far more stable and natural world than this world has ever known. A new heaven and a new earth. We must look (like John in the Apocalypse) at that great city, the holy Jerusalem, descending out of heaven from God, where the foundations are built of precious stones, the building of the wall of jasper, the gates of pearl and the streets paved with pure gold.

Read it for yourself in *Revelations* 21 and elsewhere, and doubt not that in that city is the perfection of all things including beauty, which we, in our fallen state, now dimly grope after . . .

August 11th 1971

I have now come to the end of this work. I feel for Alberti when he wrote:

The labour indeed was much more than I could have foreseen at the beginning of this undertaking. Continual difficulties every moment arose either in explaining the matter or inventing names, or methodising the subject, which perfectly confounded me, and disheartened me from my undertaking. On the other hand, the same reasons which induced me to begin this work, pressed and encouraged me to proceed. It grieved me that so many great and noble instructions of ancient authors should be lost by the injury of time, so that scarce any but Vitruvius has escaped the general wreck . . .

I observed too that those who in those days happen to undertake any new structure, generally ran after the whims of the moderns, instead of being delighted and directed by the past justness of more noble works. By this means it was plain, that this part of knowledge, and in a manner of life itself, was likely in a short time to be wholly lost. In this unhappy state of things, I could not help having it long and often in my thoughts to write upon this subject myself . . . I thought it the duty of an honest and studious mind, to endeavour to face this science, for which the most learned among the ancients had always a very great esteem, from this present ruin and oppression . . . (Book VI, Chapter I.)

Alberti tackled every department of architecture. In so far as a cat may look at a king, I have only tried to draw and describe the reasons for the parts of one particular building. But I hope to have shown in these notes, something of the wisdom and the difficulty of working in (rather than outside) the tradition.

Tradition has too long been discredited. One common objection to returning to it is that it is too easy. They say, 'You just have to copy (crib) from the pattern books etc etc'. You must be familiar with the argument. I should like to see them try. Take for example the Doric Order on this house. For various reasons we took a preference for the Renaissance Doric from Palladio rather than Scamozzi, Vignola, Sanmicheli or any other architect of that period; this in itself is a judgement about subtleties which I fear the person who has never tried will not be able to understand. But having decided on Palladio's Doric, one only finds the profile of the mouldings in his book. There are no directions given about the scale on the spacing of the columns or the snags of spacing triglyphs and metopes between them. One is not told when one can alter the rules to achieve an effect and when one can't. There is no guidance about the pros and cons of half-engaged columns as against three-quarter-engaged and their use with pilasters and so forth. But not only is there no information about the way to handle an Order or a moulding; there is no indication of the construction. If it is to be in stone, one has to decide on the size of each stone and how they will be supported. If it is in timber, a separate set of rules apply regarding shrinkage and blanketing and weathering. If the construction is not genuine and traditional the effect will soon be apparent and that effect will be appallingly amateur.

In short, one can see very quickly why the Moderns prefer to keep away from an art which has to be a labour of love. But like everything we love, we love it for a good reason. It may become a consuming passion but it never loses its interest and as we grow older our capacity to enjoy it becomes greater.

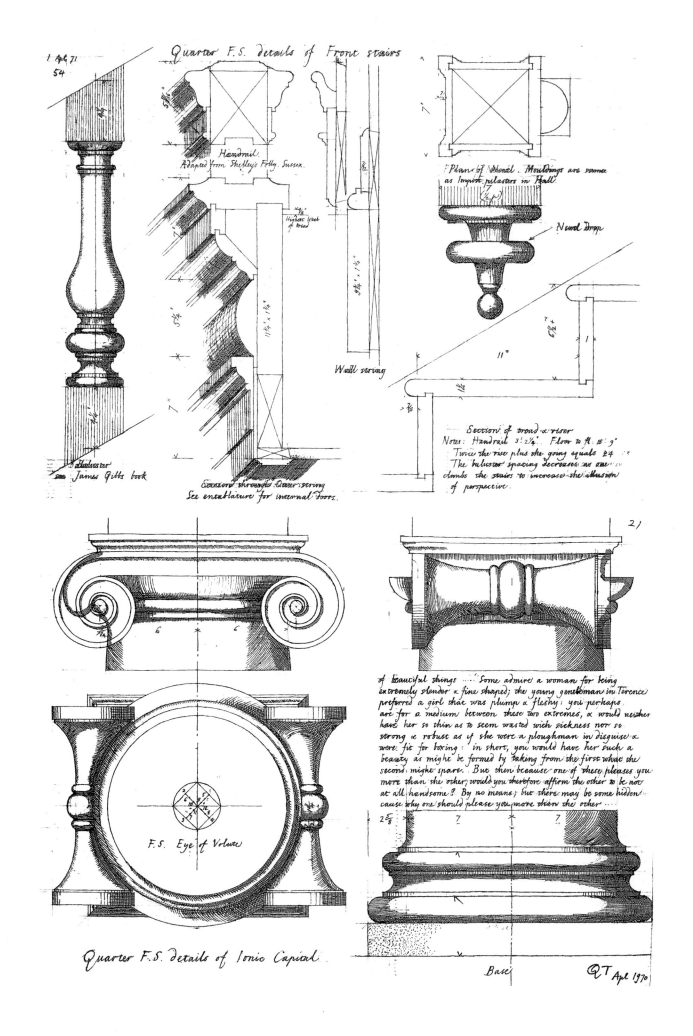

Quarter F.S. details of Front stairs

1 Apl 71
54

Handrail.
Adapted from Shelley's Folly, Sussex.

Highest level
of tread

Wall string

Baluster
see James Gibbs book

Section through Outer string
See entablature for internal doors.

Plan of Newel. Mouldings are same
as Impost pilasters in Hall.

Newel Drop

Section of tread & riser
Notes: Handrail 3' 2¼". Floor to fl. 15' 9"
: Twice the rise plus the going equals 24
: The baluster spacing decreases as one
climbs the stairs to increase the illusion
of perspective.

F.S. Eye of Volute

of beautiful things ..... Some admire a woman for being
extremely slender & fine shaped; the young gentleman in Terence
preferred a girl that was plump & fleshy: you perhaps
are for a medium between these two extremes, & would neither
have her so thin as to seem wasted with sickness nor so
strong & robust as if she were a ploughman in disguise &
were fit for boxing: in short, you would have her such a
beauty as might be formed by taking from the first what the
second might spare. But then because one of these pleases you
more than the other; would you therefore affirm the other to be not
at all handsome? By no means; but there may be some hidden
cause why one should please you more than the other ...

Quarter F.S. details of Ionic Capital.

Base

QT Apl 1970

KINGSWALDEN
HERTFORDSHIRE, 1969-71

This was the last major country house designed by Raymond Erith, and on which Terry was involved in every part of the work. It is constructed in two-inch red bricks which are bonded into solid masonry, with plain wings and a contrasting centrepiece of Doric and Ionic superimposed Orders. Palladio's rules and proportions have been followed closely, with a minimum of innovation, but with regard to the adaptation of Italian and English construction and detail, have been combined with the English detailing of Inigo Jones.

WAVERTON HOUSE
GLOUCESTERSHIRE, 1978-80

This stone house in the Cotswolds is built around a familiar 18th-century formula, that of a single central staircase lit from above and surrounded by rooms on both floors. The detailing is a combination of the stone vernacular of the Cotswolds and the bolder expression of Sanmicheli, expressed particularly in the Ionic doorcase. The use of simple whole numbers governs the plan and section throughout.

NEWFIELD
RIPON, YORKSHIRE, 1979-81

This house was constructed as the centre of a farm, following Palladio's principle that a great house is like a little city. The walls are made of stone cobbles from the Yorkshire Dales picked up from the fields around the site. The mouldings and proportions are the result of several visits to the Veneto. Although the influence of Palladio is clear, this has been combined with the characteristic attenuation of John Carr of York. The house is flanked by wings and an outer courtyard with symmetrical timber farm buildings and stables.

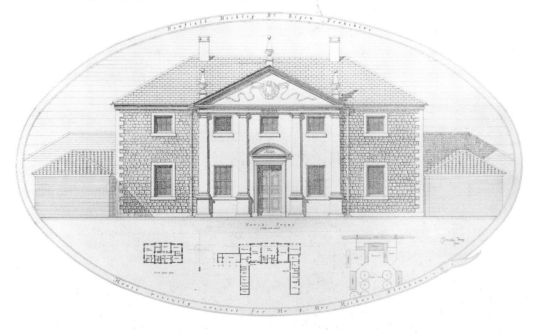

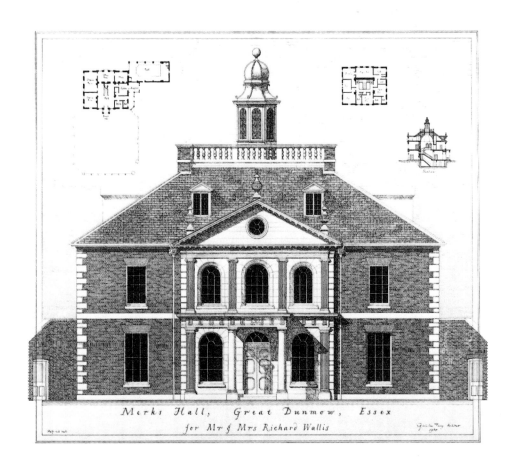

Merks Hall, Great Dunmow, Essex
for Mr & Mrs Richard Wallis

MERKS HALL
GREAT DUNMOW, ESSEX, 1984-86

This house started as a larger version of Waverton House, but was developed to make use of the local materials and methods of construction of Essex: red brick, stucco and slate. The north front employs a Doric and Ionic superimposed Order; rusticated quoins and ingeniously spaced triglyphs and modillions are positioned on a Baroque front influenced by Borromini's work at the Barberini Palace, Rome.

ABERCROMBIE RESIDENCE
KENTUCKY, USA, 1986-88

Work on this building started with the plan of Newfield, but the house is actually based on Roger Morris's design at Marble Hill, Twickenham. The house therefore has a piano nobile, *approached on the north and south by imposing staircases, and a giant Corinthian order and pediment making a centrepiece. The building is constructed from Minnesota Kasota stone, with Indiana limestone dressings.*

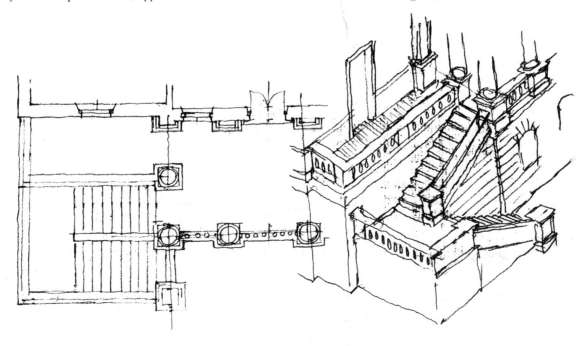

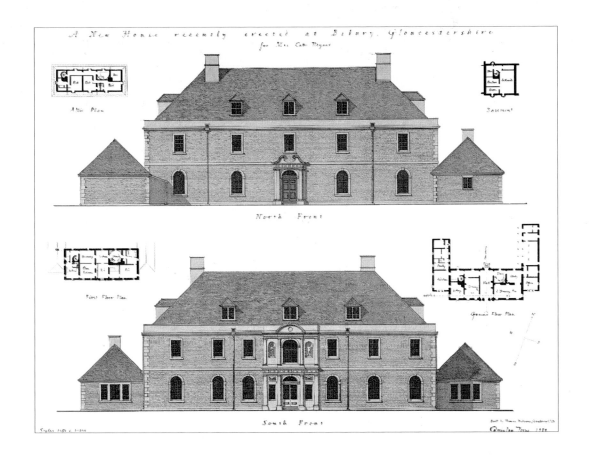

BIBURY COURT
GLOUCESTERSHIRE, 1986-88

This building has a long plan, in accordance with the requirements of the site. The detailing represents a combination of styles in which the simple classical Cotswold stone vernacular is married with the more robust classical centrepiece, which is reminiscent of Robert Smythson and the early Renaissance.

IONIC VILLA
REGENTS PARK, LONDON, 1988-90

The Ionic Villa is the first of six villas built for the Crown Estate Commissioners on the north-west corner of Regents Park, continuing the picturesque tradition established by John Nash in the early part of the 19th century.

The Ionic Villa is at the broadest end of the site and so has more depth before meeting the slope down to the Regents Canal. The plan therefore has a narrow front *with a depth unlike that of the succeeding villas. It is based on a design by Andrea Palladio for Signor Girolamo Ragona at Le Ghissole, published in the Quattro Libri. This Palladian plan has a familiar early-Georgian external treatment. The building is constructed in loadbearing brickwork, with natural and reconstructed stone dressings, and faced in stucco. The details emphasise the finer points of the Ionic Order.*

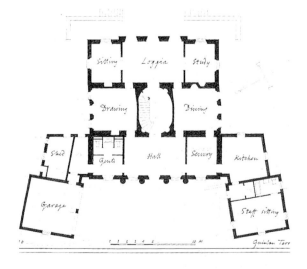

VENETO VILLA
REGENTS PARK, LONDON, 1989-91

The Veneto Villa has a wider frontage with less depth than the Ionic Villa, to take account of the different shape of the site. The plan is based on the designs by Andrea Palladio for the Villa Badoer and the Villa Zena published in the Quattro Libri, *and was thoroughly revised as the design developed.*

Whereas the Ionic Villa employs a giant Order with four columns and is massive in scale, this Villa employs a Doric Order with a superimposed Ionic Order and parapet on eight columns. The scale is therefore smaller and more refined. This is inspired by the Cornaro

Loggia in Padua by GM Falconetto, and other Palladian themes popular in the Veneto have been employed, all of which are determined by the spacing of the triglyphs and metopae in the Doric Order and the modillions in the Ionic Order. Internally the detail is English with a strong Veneto influence. Service wings provide staff accommodation, double garage and garden shed. The basement provides the normal facilities of boiler room, wine cellar, laundry, safe etc. The building is constructed in loadbearing brickwork, with natural and reconstructed stone dressings, and faced in stucco.

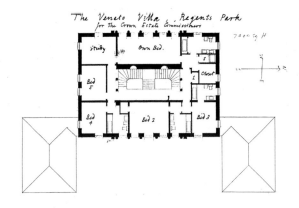

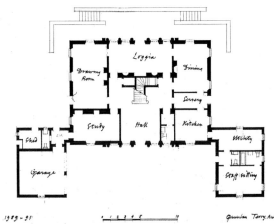

GOTHICK VILLA
REGENTS PARK, LONDON, 1989-91

The plan is based on the design by Andrea Palladio for the Villa Saraceno. It was felt that the design should develop in a more Gothick direction to reflect John Nash's preoccupation with Gothick style. The final design provides a pedimented and castellated front with Gothick Orders reminiscent of Gibbs' Temple of Liberty at Stowe, employing Batty Langley's Gothick Orders.

The inspiration for much of the detailed work was provided by Nash's Longner Hall and Combermere Abbey, Shropshire, which was one of the foremost Gothick buildings in the Strawberry Hill style, and by a number of local medieval East Anglian Churches, particularly Dedham and Higham. The balustrade to the terrace is influenced by the Palazzo Contarini-Fasan in Venice, and indeed the Venetian precedent of a Classical plan with Gothic treatment has been the main theme of the whole design.

The accommodation on the ground floor is similar to that of the Ionic and Veneto Villas but with a larger loggia overlooking the canal.

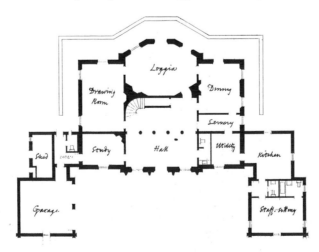

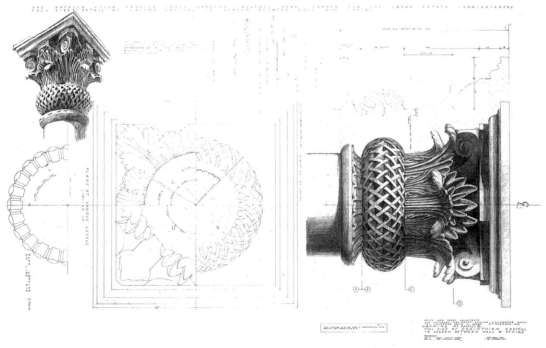

FAWLEY HOUSE
HENLEY, OXFORDSHIRE, 1988-89

This was an exercise in re-fronting an uninspiring Neo-Georgian house to exhibit some of the bolder characteristics of Baroque architecture. The window openings remained in the same position but the rusticated Tuscan and superimposed Ionic Orders break forwards and backwards to achieve a pediment within a pediment in the centrepiece and give opportunity for different finials along the parapet. It is made of Portland stone and flint.

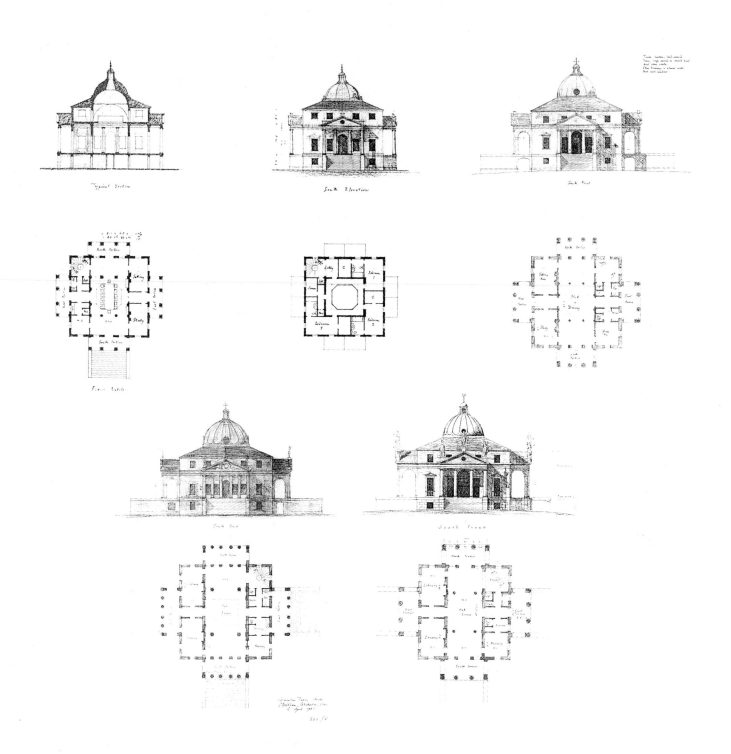

HENBURY HALL
CHESHIRE, 1982-83

This design was developed from a painting by Felix Kelly. After many revisions the completed design was worked up with all the full-size details prepared and tenders obtained. In due course the client decided to pass the whole of the work on to Julian Bicknell to make some modifications and erect the building, where many of the working drawings and stonework details appear to have been followed closely.

IV

QVARTVS
LIBER
~
URBAN
BUILDINGS
FOR
COMMERCE

MCMXCII
AD

THE RELEVANCE OF GEORGIAN ARCHITECTURE TODAY

Now imagine you are working with an intelligent and civilised developer and let us assume for sake of argument that you are working on the design of a simple building three storeys high. It is for small offices or medium-size houses and your developer has observed that the ground and first floors should have a slightly higher floor to ceiling height than the second floor; so your building, which is along a street, a rather long street, will look something like the first sketch (figure 1).

Not awfully prepossessing – it is true that it could be an office or houses but it could also be a block of flats or a health centre or a school or practically anything. It certainly reflects the three floors but the long horizontal strips of glass will obviously mean that there must be curtain walling to hide the party walls and in any event there is more glass than one needs. The building will be too hot in summer and too cold in winter. So let us improve the proportion of window to wall in order to give a more honest statement of what goes on inside the building (figure 2).

If this was a Modern building the walls would be panels of glass or concrete and the windows would be one sheet of plate glass. The roof would be flat. In all probability it would have a reinforced concrete frame structure with the necessary expansion joints at regular intervals. These could be accommodated within the horizontal and vertical joints. However, if a more permanent building is required there would be nothing to stop us making the walls of solid load-bearing brick in lime mortar. This would then overcome the problem of the expansion joint. A pitched roof would not only be a more permanent answer to avoid leaks, but we would also gain an additional floor behind the parapet without affecting the light angles. In fact we would see the logic of the Georgian terrace (figure 3).

You might feel at this point that you have achieved a very satisfactory, simple, practical and economical design. Certainly your developer would agree with the common sense in practicability and he may also appreciate the slight Georgian associations. However, he may feel, as many of us might indeed feel, that it is rather dull, particularly if the street is very long. And if the street is in an expensive (upmarket) situation he might well feel you as an architect could do more. He might well say, 'Why can't you make it more imposing and more important?' He may use various words to express his feelings but what he really means is that the building should have more style about it, more character, the sort of quality you see in old buildings – more presence. What you have designed so far could be done by any builder and the developer could save your fee by doing it himself. What he is really asking you to do is to give that building more architecture. The construction is sound; how can you now ornament the construction?

Let us therefore analyse this main front. Having filled our minds with the principles contained in the last 17 lectures, and with our sketchbooks full of architectural details that we have observed, let us study the possibilities.

Let us start by emphasising the function. There is a floor between the head of the ground floor windows and the cill of the first floor windows; this could be emphasised by a string course. There is another floor above the second floor windows which could be emphasised with a string course or possibly a cornice.

The street is very long and therefore some sort of emphasis in the centre might help to relieve the monotony. Could we not render the central two houses? And having emphasised the ground floor why not rusticate the ground floor forming a sort of podium for the first and second floors?

And having done this we could try to fit in an Order between the podium and the cornice. Of course, the size of the cornice would need to be designed to fit into the correct proportion for this Order, but let us say that we will insert the Ionic Order. It is a little too long to fit and therefore we could raise it on pedestals, but there would still be the problem of the entablature because the frieze and architrave would drop below the second floor windows. The only way round this would be to omit the architrave altogether. I don't know what you think about leaving the architrave off the Ionic Order. In fact I wonder if any of you can think of examples where an architrave has been left off for practical reasons of this sort. Your academic studies will have told you that Stuart and Revett went to Athens at the end of the 18th century and measured lots of buildings, some of which omitted the architraves. And as a result of this some architects thought they were being more scholarly and nearer to the ancient detail if they provided a cornice and frieze only. Personally, I don't think these historical observations mean very much except that they can be useful as a justification for what one has done and strangely enough they give a sort of late 18th-century look to the design because architects like Plaw and Adam were playing about in this way.

Having inserted an Ionic Order and squeezed the entablature in the way I have just described, we could then raise the pediment, which would cut across the centre dormer windows (figure 4).

The trouble about a pediment in a position like this, is that there is a pilaster on the centre line which is totally incorrect. There are no temple fronts on Classical buildings of any age – either Roman, Renaissance, or 18th century – with a column on the centre line of a pediment. All the rules for spacing of columns assume an even number of columns in the portico, so really this type of treatment should not be taken too seriously. I have only suggested this treatment to demonstrate one way in which the centre of a long, boring brick street could be treated, as it may go some way to meet the gut reaction of the man in the street and the developer that the building has more presence. The way I have suggested is very unscholarly, particularly the pediment over five columns and also the omission of the architrave, but I have worked up this example simply to show one of thousands of ways of handling a problem of this sort.

I say that it is one of thousands of ways, that it is unscholarly and that one can criticise it from an art historical point of view. But it might interest you to know that in fact it is not only a hypothetical case; it has been done before. I wonder if any of you could hazard a guess?

As you leave this building and go out of the front door into Bedford Square; look to your right, look to your left, look straight ahead. Young man go and do thou likewise.

Taken from a lecture given at the Architectural Association, Bedford Square, March 1983.

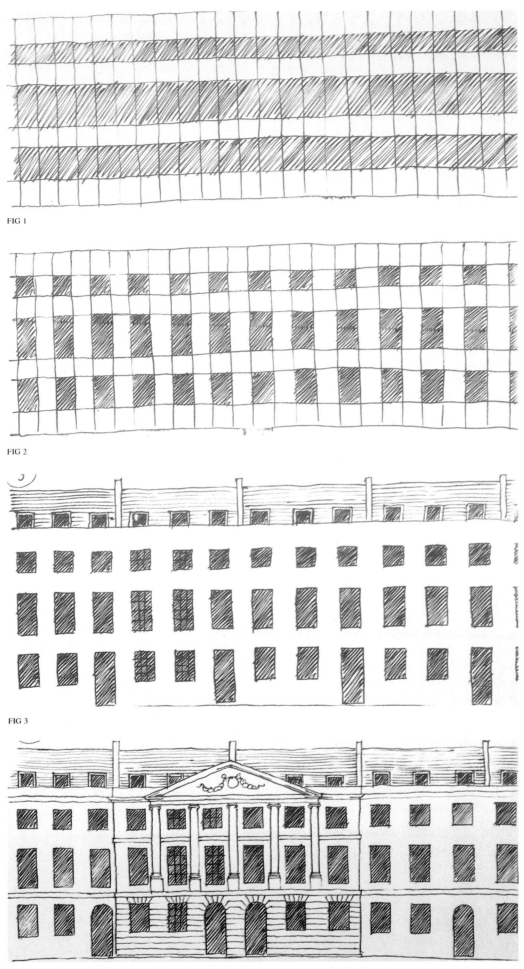

FIG 1

FIG 2

FIG 3

FIG 4

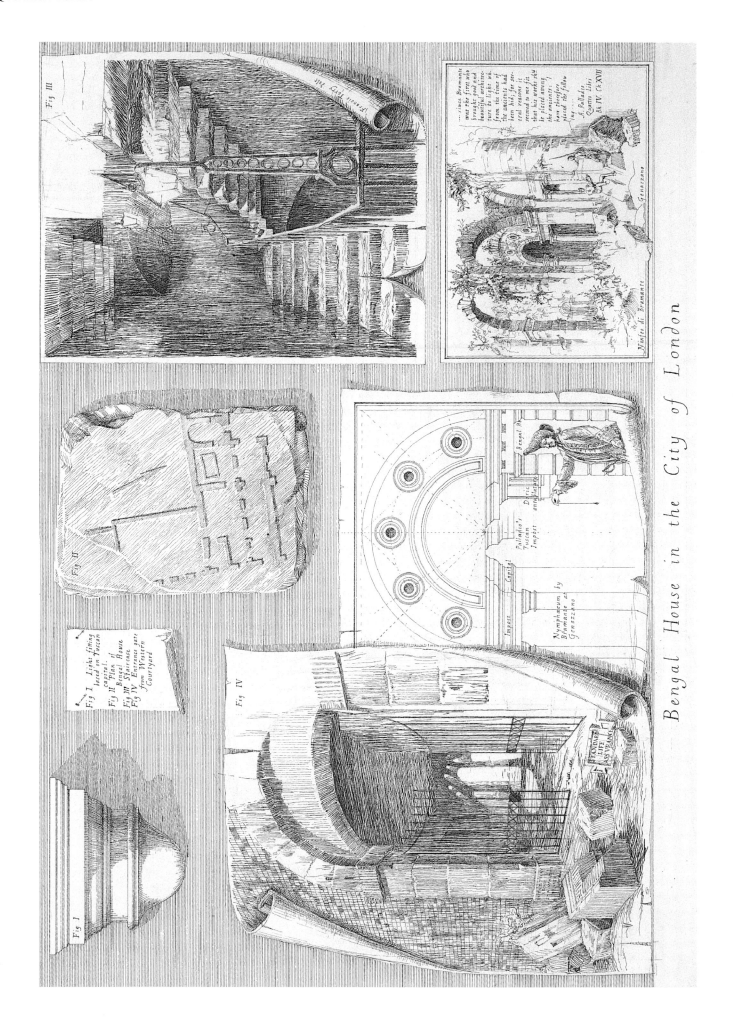

Fig III

Fig II

Fig IV

Fig I

Fig I Light fitting
based on Tuscan
capital.
Fig II Plan of
Bengal House
Fig III Staircase.
Fig IV Entrance gate
from Western
Courtyard

Bengal House in the City of London

BENGAL HOUSE
LONDON, 1983-85

This 18th-century warehouse was constructed with massive brick walls, cast-iron columns and timber floors. For historical reasons, this was the most sensitive section of the Cutlers Gardens Development. The work included converting the original warehouse space into office accommodation, with the insertion of lifts in stone surrounds and other alterations to satisfy service requirements. The main entrance is influenced by Bramante's Nymphaeum at Genazzano and is made of Portland stone.

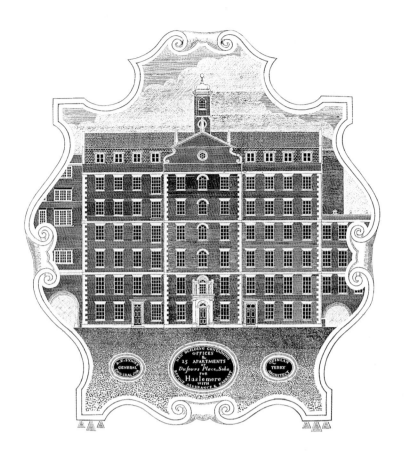

DUFOURS PLACE
WESTMINSTER, 1983-84

This building contains extensive office space and 25 flats. It is constructed in loadbearing brickwork and demonstrates the maximum height that normal traditional construction can reasonably achieve. This form of construction, and the height of six/seven storeys, was adopted throughout Europe in capital cities before the days of electric lifts and steel. This building follows an earlier design at Gray's Inn by Erith and Terry, built in 1971, for a four-storey office building with sash windows. The central door surround is influenced by late Roman trompe l'oeil perspective with motifs culled from Studio d'Architettura *by Rossi.*

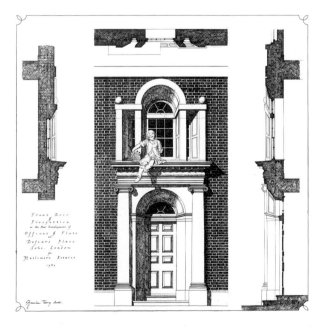

RICHMOND HOUSE
REGENT STREET, CAMBRIDGE, 1987-89

This is a modest-sized brick office building, seven windows wide, with shops on the ground floor. The sash windows reduce in height and width progressively over *the three storeys. The Doric Order positioned on the entrance to the offices is extended and adapted in timber for the shops.*

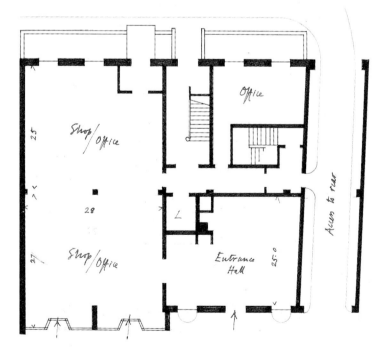

PATERNOSTER SQUARE
LONDON, 1991

This is one of two buildings proposed for the number five Cheapside site, a suggested design that shows one way in which the masterplan could be achieved. It was felt that this important site at the corner of St Paul's Churchyard and Paternoster Row should echo, in small scale, the architectural theme of the outer wall of the cathedral, which has a rusticated base and two super-imposed giant Corinthian Orders. For this reason, the south elevation facing the cathedral has a rusticated base which incorporates the office entrance and two

giant superimposed Corinthian Orders, each with two floors of offices making a five-storey building. The general lines of the architecture continue at the east end, around the corner and back along Paternoster Row. However, the pilasters are more widely spaced to allow the wide span necessary for shops on the ground floor. Because of this, the east elevation is one bay with a wide span and pilasters at the corners, and the elevation along Paternoster Row repeats this theme over four shop fronts.

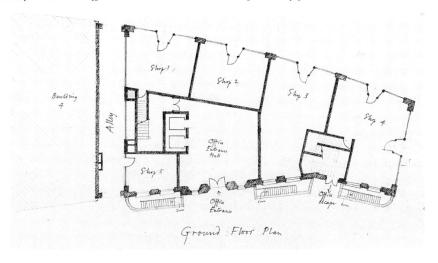

Ground Floor Plan

RICHMOND RIVERSIDE DEVELOPMENT
SURREY, 1984-87

This large comprehensive development provides offices, flats, shops, two restaurants, community facilities, two underground car parks, and riverside gardens. Two listed buildings along the riverside have been retained and re-fronted, but the rest of the development is new. It exhibits some of the rich variations of English 18th-century architecture, using red and yellow bricks, pantiles, plain tiles, slate and lead, sash and casement windows, and all the five Orders. All the office buildings are designed in accordance with the Georgian requirement of there being 20 feet from the window to the spine wall, so that it can function satisfactorily without air-conditioning or excessive artificial light –

although it was a requirement of the fund that these services should be provided and that the floor space should be marketed open plan. Work on the interiors, as with all modern office developments, is carried out after the tenant purchases the property.

In order to provide the variety that is needed on a project of this size on a sloping site, it is desirable to have many different buildings juxtapositioned, rather than one grand scheme; many of the buildings pick up the characteristic details of English and Italian architects, in particular Palladio, Longhena, Sansovino, Hawksmoor, William Chambers and the Gothic revival of the 19th century.

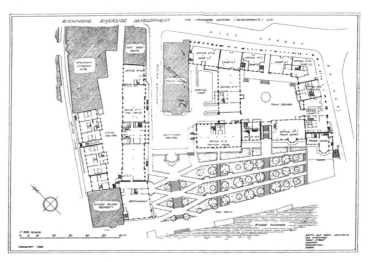

Richmond Riverside
West Gate into Town Square

QT Nov 1984

Whittaker Square: The second-floor window of the west gate was inspired by Bernini's window at Palazzo Chigi-Odescalchi. Exactly the same window was used in 18th-century England, at Beningbrough Hall. The putting to use of Italian details in this way was a notable aspect of the English 18th-century tradition; and once again it seemed appropriate that these motifs should recur in the 20th century.

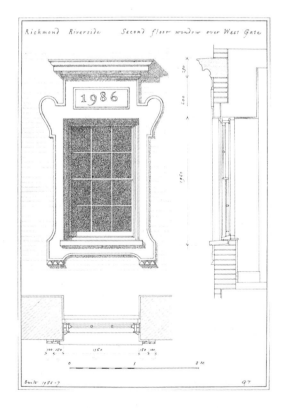

Italian Villas and Palaces of London: This forms a simplified Corinthian capital with an octagonal column shaft, forming four palm leaves and volutes on the splay with a honeysuckle pattern on the four faces, and a plain square abacus derived from Palazzo Venezia in Rome and the Basilica SS Apostoli photographed below. This is the simplest form of Corinthian capital and, together with the Venetian detail above, produces a composition which provides a relief from the more conventional treatment of the buildings to either side.

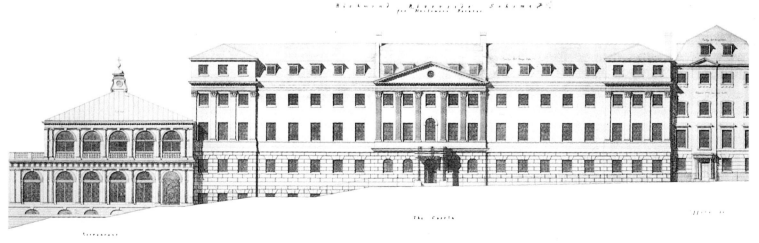

V

QVINTVS

LIBER

PUBLIC

BUILDINGS

CHURCHES

ETC.

MCMXCII
AD

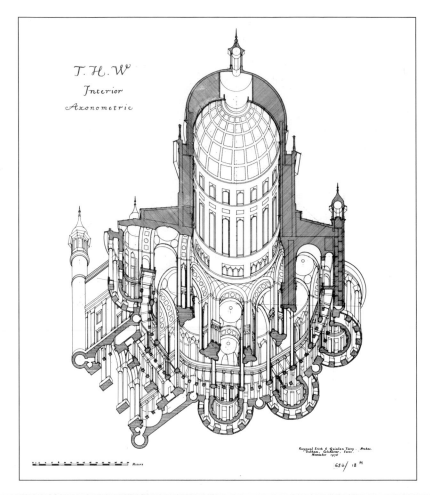

HOUSE OF WORSHIP
TEHRAN, 1972-77

The first design was the last project on which Raymond Erith worked before his death.

The second design follows the client's original instructions more closely. This project for an enormous religious building provided endless scope for the dis- *play of classical details culled from all over Italy, Spain, Venice, and the Middle East where the juxtaposition of Gothic and Classical elements in architecture was seen by the clients as an important ingredient of the expression of their beliefs.*

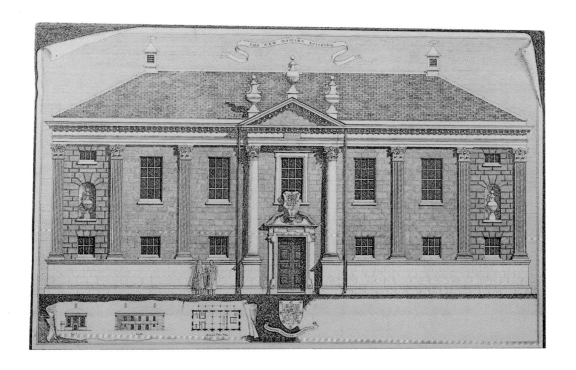

HOWARD BUILDING
DOWNING COLLEGE, CAMBRIDGE, 1985-89

This building provides a lecture theatre for 200 people and stage on the first floor with reception rooms on the ground floor. It is used for musical and dramatic performances by the university. The building is constructed in solid masonry using Portland stone for all the architectural elements including the pedestal, columns, entablature, door surrounds and finials. The walling is made in Ketton stone. There is therefore a polychrome effect similar to the Thenford summerhouse, which was part of the influence in the design. The mathematical proportion is controlled by the bot-

tom diameter of the columns and the spacing and the modillions. The intercolumniation is three at the ends, four at the sides and five in the centre; with the columns ten diameters, entablature two diameters and the modillion spacing half a diameter. The central doorcase was influenced by Longhena's door case in S Giorgio, Venice and combined with a Baroque doorcase measured in Zaragossa, Spain. It was felt that the severe Greek classicism of Wilkins called for a more lubricious Roman Baroque building dedicated to the theatre and the performing arts.

Palladio's mouldings and proportions were followed carefully, particularly in the high pedestal and bold base mouldings. Palladio's baseless Roman Doric as shown in his Quattro Libri seemed appropriate on a building which was placed so close to Grecian buildings where the baseless Doric is obligatory.

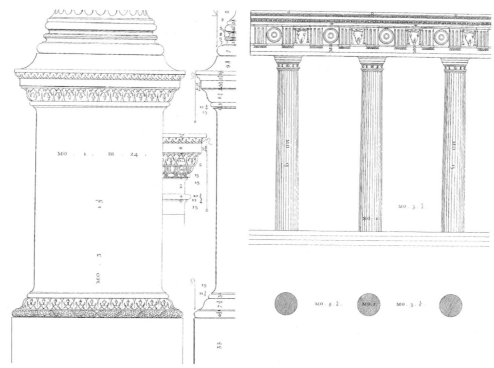

THREE STATE ROOMS
10 DOWNING STREET, LONDON, 1988-90

The restoration of the three State Drawing Rooms required the retention of three of William Kent's original fireplaces and cornices. The rest of the rooms had lost their earlier ornamentation, partly through successive incumbents and partly through bomb damage. It was therefore felt that the Kentian treatment needed to be restored. The three orders were employed in new overmantels over the three mantelpieces: Ionic for the Pillared Drawing Room with a straight pediment; coupled Doric columns for the more formal central room where guests are received; and the more delicate Corinthian order complete with swan-neck pediment for the White Room. Ornamental and enriched ceilings and door surrounds were added employing the rose, shamrock, thistle and daffodil in the four corners. These four national flowers were also worked into the rinceau frieze over the central doors which normally terminate in the figure of a man but in one instance has been modified by the tradesman to the figure of a thatcher in honour of the incumbent at that time.

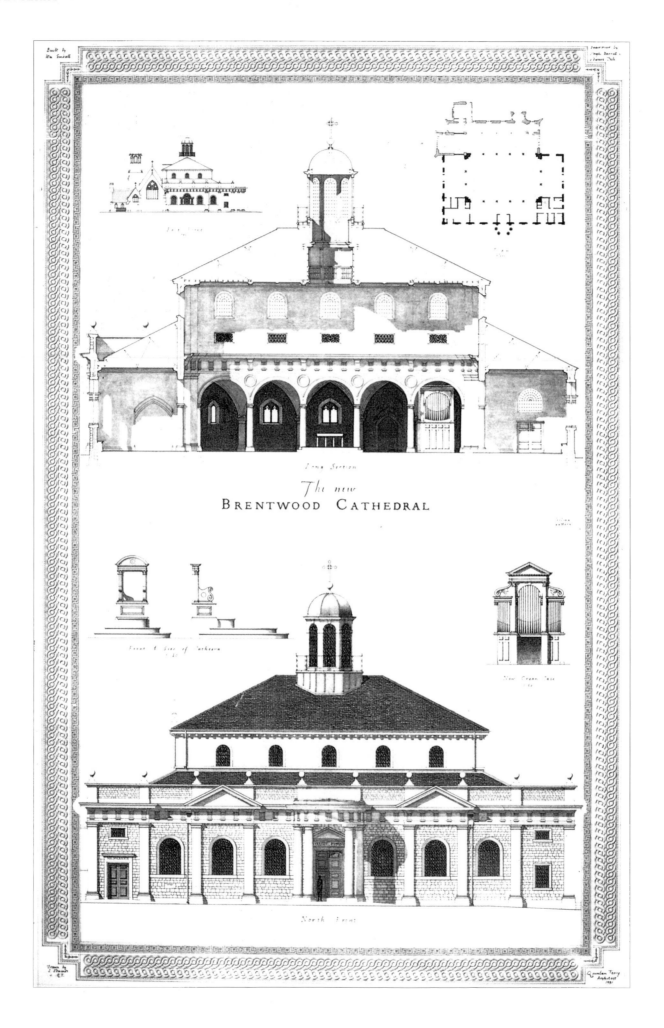

The new
BRENTWOOD CATHEDRAL

BRENTWOOD CATHEDRAL
ESSEX, 1989-91

The first building that was used as a Catholic Church on this site was an early l9th century brick building now occupied by a Social Centre. Later in the 19th century a stone Gothic Revival Building was erected. When the Church became a Cathedral it was extended by a large modern building in the 1970s built in reinforced concrete, which proved unsatisfactory. The new Cathedral replaces the 1970 building entirely and is built alongside the Gothic Revival Church to form an elongated Maltese Cross plan, the old Nave becoming the Chancel
with transepts on all four sides. In the Nave the spacing of the columns is dictated by the existing column shafts which remain on the south side but were removed in the modern extension; they have now been replaced. The arches rest on simple Tuscan columns forming an arcade supporting the whole of the central space. At the corners of this arcade are coupled giant Doric pilasters with entablature, complete with triglyphs and metopes which run round the whole of the central space; this is also the main architectural element of the exterior.

Externally, the same giant Doric order is expressed by pilasters on the north and west elevations. The centre bay of the main entrance on the north elevation forms a portico inspired by the south portico of St Paul's Cathedral and St Mary-le-Strand.

Architecturally, the inspiration is early Italian Renaissance crossed with the English Baroque of Christopher Wren. The Doric Order is Bramantesque Palladian; the arcade is obviously influenced by Brunelleschi and the cupola is inspired by Bernini's Church in Ariccia. However, the windows have characteristically English lead cames fixed to bronze saddle bars with small panes; the clerestory is faced in Smeed Dean stock brickwork, the roof is Welsh slate. The juxtaposition of classic and Gothic elements in the west elevation, and the view of Gothic arches seen through a classical arcade are inevitable in any building which has a long history.

All five Orders have been employed in the design; Tuscan for the arcade, Doric for the main giant Order, Ionic for the east and west Serlian windows, Composite and Corinthian for the organ and cathedra.

BRENTWOOD CATHEDRAL ORGAN

This new organ case has been designed around old organ pipes that were given to the Cathedral by another Church. The console forms a high pedestal which supports a giant Corinthian Order with pediment in the centre. The impost to this Order is a minor Corinthian Order complete with entablature and half pediments; a characteristic Basilica front used frequently by Palladio in numerous Churches in Venice.

ST MARY'S PADDINGTON ORGAN
LONDON, 1976

This organ, which was built in memory of Raymond Erith, was inspired by the designs of the late-Georgian organ builder GP England of Wareham and Blandford Forum, in Dorset. This seemed entirely appropriate at St Mary's Church, Paddington Green, which was built by Plaw in 1791.

Maitland Robinson Library

A Tower of the Winds
B Choragic Monument of Thrasyllus, Athens
C Portico of Augustus
D Medici Chapel, Florence
E Osberton House, Notts
F Fitzwilliam Museum, Cambridge

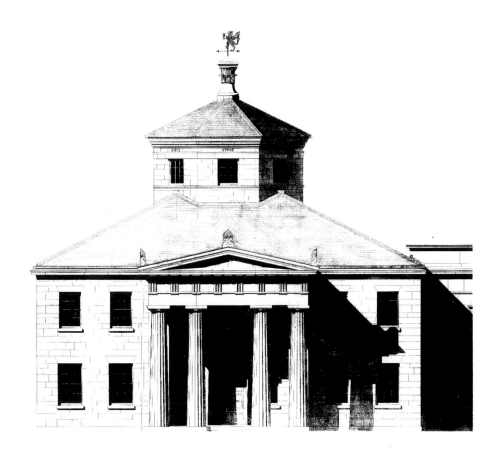

MAITLAND ROBINSON LIBRARY
DOWNING COLLEGE, CAMBRIDGE, 1990-92

This new library is built on the principle that the books are stacked in the centre of the plan with the carrells arranged under the windows. Thus a square building is formed with a central octagonal staircase providing access between the basement, ground and first floors. With the college's commitment to classicism from Wilkins onwards and the strong emphasis on the Greek Revival, it was felt appropriate that this building should form a 'capriccio' of the outstanding monuments of the Acropolis. For that reason the Portico of Augustus forms the main entrance and south portico of the building; the Choragic monument of Thrasyllus forms the East Portico; and the Tower of the Winds forms the octagonal cupola, which

has a Greek Corinthian capital at the apex with a weathervane. The Greek names for the eight winds are inscribed on each of the eight faces of the octagon.

The whole building is made in natural Ketton stone in loadbearing construction. Each of the metopae has been carved to symbolise tripos subjects that are taught in the college.

The entrance doorcase is a combination of Greek work with splayed architraves combined with Michelangelo's doorcase at the Medici Chapel, Florence where the reduction in width of the architrave and fine detail foreshadow the change in taste from the Roman to Greek detail.

The acroterion on the apex and springing of the main pediment to the south portico is carved in Ketton stone based on the measurements of original Greek details, *with particular reference to the drawings of Inwood, Stuart and Revett, and William Wilkins.*

South front near completion: The metopae in the frieze symbolise academic subjects from left to right, starting at the east end: the Trinitarian eye in a sunburst over the open Bible with the words ἐν ἀρχη ἠν λογος for theology; the lyre for music; the Tower of Babel for languages; the globe for geography; the brazen serpent for medicine; the laurel wreath for English; the scales for law; the DNA double helix for biology and genetics; the hourglass for history; the radio telescope for astronomy and physics; the Athenian owl for the classics; the compasses and set square for architecture; the icosahedron for chemistry and mathematics.

OPERA HOUSE
GIFFORD, EDINBURGH, 1992

Gian Carlo Menotti, the founder of the Spoleto and Charleston Festivals, wishes to build a theatre school on the site of the stables at Yester. This design provides for an opera house with a capacity of up to 400 spectators. There are four galleries and a pit similar to the Ciao Mellisa at Spoleto. The castellated Classicism seen in design of the Doric portico and fly tower is reminiscent of the work of William and Robert Adam; this is particularly appropriate as they were also involved in Yester House.

THE ORIGIN OF THE ORDERS

The theme of this essay is the origin of the Classical Orders. The subject is very subjective and speculative, and I do not expect the reader to accept all I have to say – my aim is not so much to convince as to draw attention to the fact that the appearance of Classical buildings does something to people.

The sight of the portico and dome of the Pantheon does something to me. I think of the aspirations of the people who paid for it and admire their priorities. I think of the enthusiasm and skill of the architects, the organisation of the builders in erecting so many columns weighing about a hundred tons each! I think of the sheer pleasure it must have given the thousands of workmen, the masons and carvers, bricklayers, carpenters and smiths who worked together to produce such fine detail. One also thinks that over the last 2,000 years, that portico has given a silent testimony of a great age to succeeding generations. It has had an effect on everybody (every thinking person) who has seen it. It has reminded them of what civilised man can produce. It is significant that the aspirations of civilised man have been expressed through the geometrical and naturalistic forms of the Classical Orders. They seem to echo some deep longing in the soul and one wonders where they have come from, and who was the genius who invented such a timeless and universal recipe for architecture.

Indeed, the Orders have so many humanly inexplicable characteristics that it is hard to imagine that they came about as a result of human ingenuity or accident of time. Everything about them indicates the work of the same Mind 'who created the Heavens and Earth and all that is in them . . .' In common with Nature, the Orders fill man with awe and admiration. Like Nature they have survived unchanged from their very beginning and their origin still remains a mystery.

They can, in a most extraordinary way, express all historical periods, national characteristics, political systems and even personal moods of individual architects, yet preserve their principles and remain neutral.

Again, totally inexplicably, Classical buildings give those who use them a sense of privilege and discipline which makes for a satisfied and organised existence, so different from the discontented laissez-faire attitude of the present world.

Privilege and discipline are anathema to this age, as indeed are faith and worship. But I can only explain the phenomenon of Classical Orders as a direct consequence of the fact that first and foremost they were ordained to contain the visible manifestation of human worship of the only true God. It does not take a fanatical believer to see this – any intelligent man who has worked with, and understood, Classical principles of architecture, will sooner or later admit the sense of wonder and mystery that surrounds them. My late partner and mentor Raymond Erith was not a man of orthodox beliefs but he believed very strongly that the essence of Classical architecture, and the Orders in particular, were 'given' at some point in history:

The Classical Orders of architecture: by that I mean the Doric, Ionic and Corinthian Orders (and you can add the Tuscan and the Composite if you wish, as an elaboration of the Doric and Corinthian), are so perfect in their proportions and detail and application to the art of building, that they

could not have been invented by man. There is, to me, only one satisfactory explanation of their origin and that is that they are divinely inspired.

Erith used to say this and I found it not surprising that the earliest description of the Orders known to man comes in the second book of the Bible, written some 3,500 years ago by the divinely inspired hand of Moses. It is in the book of *Exodus* that he records in detail his commission from God to erect the Tabernacle in the Wilderness for His worship and honour.

To my mind, the first time the three Orders appeared in a recognisable form was in this Tabernacle.

Moses spent 40 days in Mount Sinai receiving the Law and the pattern of all the details of the Tabernacle direct from God. The moral law contained in the Ten Commandments distinguished the people of God from the rest of the world and has continued – through to the Christian church to this day – unaltered. The ceremonial law, giving detailed instructions about worship and sacrifice, was the clearest guide to the children of Israel until it was fulfilled in the Son of God and continues to this day a demonstration of His high-priestly work and sacrificial atonement. Furthermore, the visual form of the building in which the one true God was to be worshipped could not be left to the vain imagination of man; so a detailed description was given to Moses. It seems that the distinctive pattern of these Orders has continued in some form on all civilised public buildings until the beginning of the century.

Moses, a natural genius, was uniquely qualified to receive these instructions and his learning in the Egyptian court enabled him to understand and describe the construction and detail of the building. Not only was the architectural detail described by Moses from the pattern he was shown in the Mount; but a craftsman and an artist were needed to put ornament and enrichment into such a building. We read of two men, Bezaleel and Aholiab, of whom it is said:

God has filled them with the Spirit of God in wisdom, in understanding and in knowledge and in all manner of workmanship; and to devise curious works, to work in gold, and in silver, and in brass, and in the cutting of stones, to set them, and in carving of wood, to make all manner of cunning work. (*Exodus*, Chapter 35, verses 31-33.)

These two men must have been among the most outstanding artists of all time, and it would seem that they were inspired through the Holy Spirit to formalise and sanctify the natural shapes of the creation for future generations to copy. Thus a green branch of a palm tree, cut off and driven into the ground to act as a post, will often sprout leaves; these would then be formalised into the capital of a column. Or a rope tied around the top and bottom of such a post to stretch sheets and tents would become a base with bead and fillet mouldings.

The plan of the Tabernacle indicates the division into the Court, the Holy place and the Holy of Holies, all in accordance with the measurements given in *Exodus*, Chapters 36 and 37.

The origin of the Doric Order as used in the Court of the Tabernacle: Acacia (shittim) wood would have been used for the columns. These were five cubits high with silver capitals with hooks and fillets and bases of brass. They supported a pole on which curtains were stretched and they would have had guy ropes inside and outside to hold them upright. There must have been many primitive canvas enclosures erected on this principle which Bezaleel and Aholiab would have formalised into a simple Order with capital and base. This Order would have been known to King David and passed on to his son Solomon who further elaborated it in the colonnade around the outer court of the Temple in Jerusalem. These colonnades were covered and a simple form of roof construction is shown employing the essential parts of a simple roof elaborated slightly to show the possible origin of the parts of the Doric entablature. Thus the beam (or architrave) supports simple trusses with tie beams showing their exposed ends (triglyphs) which are dowelled to the top fillet (or tenia) of the beam with pegs (or guttae). The principal rafter of the truss supports purlins and plates in the normal way, which in turn support common rafters with their ends exposed (mutules) and are finished with a tilting fillet (cyma recta) under the eaves.

The origin of the Ionic Order as used at the door of the Holy Place of the Tabernacle: the sprouting palm branch mentioned earlier would form leaves which would press up under the square top, or abacus, and curl downwards in volutes at the corners. This natural curvature would appeal to the two inspired artists, particularly as they could be formalised and sanctified into the curvature of the horns of a ram. These were then made in acacia and overlaid with gold, with gold capitals and brass bases. They were placed in the eminently suitable position at the door of the Tabernacle, thus reminding the worshippers how they must approach God. They would be reminded of Abraham's sacrifice of a ram in the place of Isaac and that God would also accept them through the same sacrifice. It would print on their minds the fundamental teaching, that without the shedding of blood there is no remission of sins.

Once again King David, always aware of his need of forgiveness, would very probably have left instructions in his plans for the Temple in Jerusalem that this voluted capital should be placed on the top of the columns at the entrance to the Holy Place.

The origin of the Corinthian Order: the leaves of the sprouting palm branch already mentioned could make a variation in the arrangement of the leaves below the abacus. Once again this arrangement, which is more intricate and decorative than the previous Order, would be formalised in acacia and overlaid in gold, with gold capitals and silver bases, and placed either side of the entrance to the Holy of Holies in the Tabernacle where it supports the veil.

Once again Solomon, with his love of beauty and refinement would have developed this still further, not only inside the Temple but also on the two columns, Jachim and Boaz, which were placed in front of the Temple. These were described as follows:

And he made two chapiters of molten brass, to set upon the tops of the pillars: the height of the one chapiter was five cubits (7ft 6in or thereabouts) . . . and nets of checkerwork, and wreaths of chainwork, for the chapiters which were upon the top of the pillars; . . . and he made the pillars and two rows round about upon the one network, to cover the chapiter that were upon the top, with pomegranates . . . and the chapiters that were upon the top of the pillars were of lily-work. And the chapiters upon the two pillars also above, over against the belly which way by the network. (*I Kings*, Chapter 7, verses 16-22.)

This description is a little hard to illustrate and one wonders whether the writer is describing a superimposed Order in the Temple as well. However, it is significant that this description refers to 'nets of checkerwork' and 'the belly'. The nets of checkerwork call to mind the basketwork, said to be drawn by Callimachus and described by Vitruvius. The belly refers to the geometrical shape of the Corinthian capital which is an upturned bell (or belly) supporting a square horned abacus.

Theologians of every persuasion agree that this Temple building was derived directly from the Tabernacle in the Wilderness. Not only are the plan measurements of the Temple exactly twice the size of the Tabernacle in all its main dimensions, but the divisions into Court, Holy Place and Holy of Holies are identical. The purpose of these two buildings was the same, only the materials and scale were different. The Tabernacle was a portable timber structure (albeit extensively covered in gold) to be used while the Israelites were settled in the promised land. It was built around 1000BC with its Corinthian capitals which set the style for the surrounding nations, and was the envy of the ancient world.

The story of the Queen of Sheba making her long journey from the south in order to see the beauty and grandeur of that Temple is well known and recorded (*II Chronicles*, Chapter 9, verse 1, etc) and yet even the Queen of Sheba had to admit that what she saw was far greater than the description she had heard before she came. Barely 50 years after the Temple's completion it is recorded that:

In the fifth year of King Rehoboam (Solomon's son) Shishak,
King of Egypt came up against Jerusalem . . . and took away
the treasures of the King's house. (*II Chronicles*, Chapter 12.)

It is therefore probable that the distinctive feature and ornaments of this famous building were copied and repeated in Egypt. Shishak was a great builder as well as conqueror. He built, restored and improved many Temples and his name is associated with those at Karnak and Luxor. It is interesting that until that time (945BC) there is little ornament in Egyptian architecture: the purest geometrical forms such as the pyramid, obelisk and post and lintel seem to prevail. It was Solomon who first put up free-standing columns with capitals rather than obelisks in important places.

Solomon's Temple was destroyed by the Babylonians in 588BC, but just over half a century later Darius, King of Persia, was building his palace at Persepolis (521BC). To this day one may see at Persepolis fluted columns with entasis, bearing witness to earlier detail than the Greek. There are also moulded bases and carved capitals curiously reminiscent of Solomon's 'rams' horns' and 'nets of checkerwork'. There are stone doorways complete with architraves and entablatures enriched with beads and reels and lily-work. Darius was a son or grandson of Cyrus who had such veneration for Solomon's Temple that he decreed that the captive Jews should return to Jerusalem to rebuild it.

At that time when such sophisticated classicism was practised at Persepolis, the Greeks knew only a most primitive version of Doric, such as can be seen on the 6th century BC Temples at Paestum. There is no enrichment of mouldings but curiously enough the earliest Temple has a five column front as had the entrance of Moses's Tabernacle. Alexander's conquest of Persia in 332BC obviously had a great effect on Greek architecture and the ideas of Persepolis soon found their way to Athens.

It is universally accepted, and indeed confirmed in writing by Vitruvius, that the Romans acquired all their ideas on architecture from Greece. By this time, over 1,500 years after the building of the Tabernacle in the Wilderness and after several sackings of Jerusalem, which reduced the once prosperous and influential Jewish nation to a persecuted minority, all trace of the true origins of the Orders would have disappeared and Vitruvius would have had a free hand to construct a theory which suited him and his superiors.

Vitruvius was a military engineer under Julius Caesar in the African War (46BC) and inspector of military machines under Augustus, to whom he dedicated his book *De Architectura* (completed *c*16-13BC). It would not be hard to argue that as a good party-line Roman, he felt compelled to give authority to the religious basis behind the Imperial architecture. His dedication is revealing:

. . . while your divine intelligence and will, Imperator Caesar, was engaged in acquiring the right to command the world, and while your fellow citizens, when all their enemies had been laid low by your invincible valour, were glorying in your triumph and victory, while all foreign nations were in subjection awaiting your beck and call, and the Roman people and senate, released from their alarm, were beginning to be guided to your most noble conceptions and policies, I hardly dared, in view of your serious employments, to publish my writings . . .

In Book IV, chapter I, Vitruvius gives a fanciful account of the origins of the Doric, Ionic and Corinthian Orders. No reasons are given for the distinctive features of each Order, except the Corinthian capital, which he elegantly describes as follows:

A free-born maiden of Corinth, just of marriageable age, was attacked by an illness and faded away. After her burial, her nurse, collecting a few little things which used to give the girl pleasure while she was alive, put them in a basket, carried it to the tomb, and laid it on top thereof, covering it with a roof-tile so that the things might last longer than in the open air. This basket happened to be placed just above the root of an acanthus. The acanthus root, pressed down meanwhile though it was by the weight, when springtime came round put forth leaves and stalks in the middle, and the stalks, growing up along the sides of the basket, and pressed out by the corners of the tile through the compulsion of its weight, were forced to bend into volutes at the outer edges. Just then Callimachus whom the Athenian admired for the refinement and delicacy of his artistic work, passed by the tomb and observed the basket with the tender young leaves growing round it. Delighted with the novel style and form he built some columns after that pattern for the Corinthians, determined their symmetrical proportions, and established from that time forth the rules to be followed in finished works of the Corinthian Order . . .

That Vitruvius was seriously and impartially interested in knowing the origins of the Orders is unlikely; he was a party man. That he knew that there were other beliefs about the origins of the Imperial style contained in the Holy Book of the detested and insubordinate nation of the Jews, is possible. That he knew about the rebuilding of Solomon's Temple by Herod at the time of his writing is probable and he may well have visited it on one of his military expeditions. If one reads the contemporary accounts in Josephus about the size and scale and materials and beauty of the rebuilt Temple in Jerusalem, it seems strange indeed that Vitruvius should omit any reference to that building, or of the Jews or their history, particularly when he says so much about the surrounding nations.

We have examples today of powerful regimes with a strong ideological basis attempting to rewrite the history books, and it would appear that Vitruvius was attempting to make people think that the Imperial style was rooted in the Imperial religion. Thus, he named the three Orders after the Greek regions of Doria, Ionia and Corinth. He not only attempted, but succeeded. His book was practically the only written work on architecture to be preserved and was avidly taken up in the Renaissance by the Italians.

And so the Orders have survived as each successive empire has waxed and waned. They have been revived after periods of darkness. They will be revived again after this period of darkness has ended. It is characteristic of all God-given truth that it survives through most adverse circumstances and is propagated by an insignificant minority.

Who would credit a dozen uneducated fishermen led by a penniless carpenter, with the establishment of the universal Church against which no earthly powers can prevail?

Similarly, who would believe that an obscure shepherd leading a band of wandering exiles through the Wilderness of Arabia should devise the perfect set of architectural principles which survived worldwide, through all man-made fashions and conceits?

But God hath chosen the foolish things of the world to confound the wise; and God hath chosen the weak things of the world to confound the things which are mighty . . . that no flesh should glory in His presence.

And so to God only wise be glory through Jesus Christ for ever. Amen.

Origin of the Orders won the £5,000 European Prize in 1982 from the Philippe Rotthier Foundation. Published by Archives d'Architecture Moderne *No 26, 1984 and by the* Architectural Review, *February 1983.*

SEVEN MISUNDERSTANDINGS ABOUT CLASSICAL ARCHITECTURE

I try to practise as a Classical architect today, and I enjoy it. I have come to this position not by listening to lectures or intellectual arguments (because it is not primarily an academic subject), but by working for eleven years side by side with a great architect, Raymond Erith RA, who died in 1973.

In the past, architectural students started as apprentices working in offices and coming together in the evenings to discuss their ideas, which they had picked up from their masters and the practical world around them. Today, the modern system of architectural education requires that students spend five years full-time in academic theory, before being allowed out to start forming a theory based on practical experience. It is possibly because of this process of indoctrination that students often ask questions of a theoretical kind which do not relate to the practical world and the art of building. It is this relationship between theory and practice that cause frequent misunderstandings about the relevance of Classical architecture.

There are many ways in which Classical architecture is misunderstood and the theme of this paper is based on seven of the more frequent misunderstandings. These concern the following subjects: Pastiche; Functionalism; New building types; Materials; Cost; Tradesmen; and Politics.

Let us start with the *first misunderstanding*. A popular misconception is that Classical architecture is pastiche. It is often said that it is a simple matter of cribbing from the pattern books. I notice that many art historians are full of this and like all people who are protected from reality they will never learn until they start to practise. I believe there is something in the Gospels: 'If you know these things, happy are ye if ye do them'. It is only in the doing that we learn.

For instance, say you are asked to design a door in the Palladian manner. You turn to Palladio's *Quattro Libri* and you find that you are only given the profile of the moulding. No guidance is given on size, scale, materials or methods of construction. Even if you can decide on a door three feet six inches wide by seven feet high, with architraves one-sixth of the opening and an entablature above, how do you relate it to the wall? How do you convert these lines of an engraving into building materials?

You are now faced with decisions about the lining, frame, door and its panelling, not to mention the treatment of the surround on the other side of the wall. To do this you have to draw on your knowledge and experience and the result will express a number of architectural subtleties. If you are not careful, you may also express your own shortcomings and lack of skill! If you feel that a door of this sort is not sufficiently important for its position you can add an Order either side, and even a pediment.

This leads to the *second misunderstanding* which concerns functionalism. It is said that in a democratic age, the greater or lesser importance of such a simple thing as a door is no longer relevant. Quite apart from the democracy question, every large municipal building has to serve different groups of people and it is helpful if the main public entrance is easily distinguished from the office staff entrance or the door to the refuse collection. Even in the sitting room of a small house the door to the hall or kitchen should be more important than the door to a cupboard. The old rules relating to the relative importance (the hierarchy) of doors and their architraves still apply and fulfil an important function. If they are well understood they help the client use the building, and if ignored, as they are in most modern buildings, you have to resort to signs and symbols to guide the public in the right direction.

We therefore see just one of the functions of mouldings in stressing the relative importance of different doors. It amazes me that mouldings which are so simple can lead to such infinite variations. After all there is really only one curve and one straight. A cavetto is a concave curve whilst an ovolo is the opposite. A cyma recta is a cavetto followed by an ovolo, whereas a cyma reversa is the opposite. The fillets merely come between. If you stack them together, they say something – maybe an Ionic modillion cornice.

You may ask, 'What is the reason for the sequence of these mouldings?' The answer is that they have come about as the result of many causes like weathering, building construction over thousands of years, historical precedent and other influences. But probably most important is sciagraphy, or the science of casting shadows.

If we draw the lines of perspective we can see how the profiles of the mouldings are picked out by the shadows. The front of the corona and the modillions are in direct sunlight, whereas the curves of the cymas and ovolos come into and go out of shadow gently. You might think that the soffit and the coffers are lost because they are in complete shadow. But strangely enough, the abacus on top of the capital acts as a reflector and sends a soft light up into the coffers by reflection. Similarly, on a Tuscan capital the square abacus casts a shadow on the circular shaft below. It also causes a flash of light on the top of the echinus and expresses the shape. A combination of soft and hard shadows is brought about by the simple geometrical solids of square abacus supported by circular echinus.

We have been thinking of the play of light, the light of the sun, on the simplest geometrical solids. It gives pleasure to the eye and makes us feel good. Simple pleasures caused by natural things and in no way dependent on artificial light and the consumption of energy or the world's resources. Classical architecture comes from a natural world which valued light and air more highly than we do today because there was then no artificial light or ventilation to help one out of difficulties.

Therefore, in planning a small house it is common sense to put the front door in the middle with the hall and stairs behind it. Thus there would be a sitting room on one side and a kitchen on the other. The windows would come in the middle of the rooms, with the area of glazing a little over one-tenth of the floor area, making the building neither too cold in winter nor too hot in summer. One might also splay the reveals to soften the light as it came into the room. The chimneys could be at the ends under the gable and the roof would, of course, be pitched. The first floor would be much the same, with two bedrooms and a cupboard on the landing. The elevation would be a functional and natural reflection of the plan.

This is a simple example of a well-proved plan, used for centuries and still hard to beat on functional grounds alone. It is capable of infinite variations and additions so that it can in modern times easily accommodate a bathroom on the first floor, or be extended to accommodate additional rooms on the ground floor. Thus it is a method of building that can adapt itself thoroughly to change without sacrificing its principle.

This brings us to the *third misunderstanding*, which concerns new types of buildings. How can you, some ask, expect airports, multi-storey car parks, factories and office blocks to be part of the Classical tradition?

I will admit that the architect has no ready-made answer and will have to do a lot of thinking. But had Bramante not thought hard about the juxtaposition of the circular pagan temple with an early Christian basilica, we might not have known the Renaissance church typified by St Peter's. Bramante approached a new problem along the well-travelled lines of Classical principles and he produced an entirely new and highly successful type of building. Is there not an opportunity and a challenge today to approach each new problem from old principles rather than from a childish desire to produce an elevation hitherto unknown?

In fact, every problem, even a conservatory on the side of a house, is a new problem. The architectural result depends entirely upon what is in the mind of the designer. I will say more about what is in the mind of the designer later on.

The *fourth misunderstanding* is about materials. I am often asked why I do not use modern materials. To answer this let us first make two short lists, of old and new building materials respectively: Old: limestone; marble; lime concrete; clay bricks and tiles; slates; sandstone. New: Portland cement concrete; steel; reinforced concrete; reconstructed stone; pre-cast concrete; sandlime bricks; stainless steel; aluminium; laminated plastics.

Now I am no obscurantist and I admit that I have specified at various times the materials on the second list, but I have nearly always done so because they are cheaper in the short term. There is little doubt that quite apart from their appearance and cheapness, the materials in the second list have a shorter life than those in the first. This means that if you use them you will have higher maintenance costs than with the traditional materials. There are the notorious examples like roofing felt which now has a shorter guarantee than most refrigerators, but leaving that aside it is worth noting that Hope Bagenal, who was for many years head of the Building Research Station, pointed out that the best building materials are practically inert, whereas the great defect of all modern materials is their high coefficient of expansion.

This means that their seasonal and diurnal expansion and contraction is such that expansion joints are essential. Even a modern brick wall has to have expansion joints every 30 feet. This in turn breaks up the monolithic nature of any structure into little isolated blocks with expansion joints. The weathering and attrition of these joints is an obvious long-term weakness, whereas a traditionally built structure has none of these problems, as the matrix is lime instead of cement. Think of the Pantheon in Rome, built in brick and lime mortar. It has a diameter of 142 feet and has stood for nearly 2,000 years. No reinforced concrete structure would last as long because once air and moisture have penetrated to the reinforcement there is nothing which can permanently inhibit its breakdown. It does not even make a good ruin!

Of course modern materials (materials with high coefficients of expansion) have their uses for temporary buildings like exhibition halls and factories, but all too often their cheapness has been their main attraction.

This is really the point about the *fifth misunderstanding* which concerns cost; for any equation which involves cost must also be related to maintenance and permanence. If cheapness has been properly equated in relation to the life of a building, the client would normally prefer the permanent solution. A caravan may be cheaper than a well-built house, but in 20 years time (when the mortgage is paid off) the house has appreciated, whereas the caravan has only scrap value. It is this form of short-term economics which has too often been accepted as the reason against more traditional solutions.

We have built a large office building in London in traditional materials and construction. It had to be traditional for conservation reasons and the client was prepared to pay more for it, but in fact it cost slightly less per square foot than comparable office buildings at the time. Furthermore, because it had a Georgian proportion of window to wall it did not require air-conditioning and thereby reduced the running cost considerably.

The modern client not only needs a deep pocket and a short memory, but he also needs an inordinate supply of combustible fuel to keep the building properly serviced. In the past, the resources of the earth were scarce and the buildings reflected a sense of moderation which is altogether lacking in the overglazed facades with which we are so familiar today. The real question is whether or not the designed article is good value for money.

Value for money. This brings us to the *sixth misunderstanding* which is about tradesmen. People ask, 'How can you find men to do your class of work these days?' As if men no longer can, or want to, produce skilled work. The truth is that whenever there is good work to be done there are men to do it. We have never had difficulty in obtaining first-class joinery. We prepare full-size details and specify the quality and provided a reputable builder is doing the work it normally needs no further explanation. The same goes for plasterers, bricklayers, slaters, stonemasons and even woodcarvers and coppersmiths. Generally, I find that the more intricate the detail, the more willing the tradesmen are to take on the work.

I think the working man is misunderstood by everyone, not least himself. There is, after all, no fundamental difference between the tradesman, the architect or his employers. They are all men made in the image of God with needs and aspirations. But I have noticed that we are all far less covetous when we are working on a job we enjoy. At the end of the day we can go home and think about it and return the next day to take the work a little further. I have heard this from so many tradesmen, that it must be true. It is the boredom of repetitive work, work which requires nothing from you, that makes for an empty mind. The empty mind is a dangerous thing because it soon gets filled with a host of other thoughts which no industrial expert can control – and this brings me to the last of the misunderstandings.

The *seventh misunderstanding* is about political implications. It is often said that there are political implications in the Classical style: that because Mussolini used it in one form it is an expression of fascism; or because it was adopted in Moscow for a time after the Revolution it is an expression of socialism. The truth is that it does express the society that uses it, just as a man's or woman's face expresses what is in their heart, but this does not mean that it takes sides. Historically, it has been the expression of such diverse political and religious systems as Republican and Imperial Rome, the capitalist Medicis in Florence, the corrupt Borgia popes, the Baroque spiritualism of Michelangelo, the Protestant Reformation in Palladian England, the Counter-Reformation in Rococo Bavaria and Spain, the God-fearing simplicity of the Nonconformists in England and America, and the overbearing conceit of the Victorians. Although the spiritual, political, material and temporal influences are crystallised in wood and stone and expressed in Classical forms, the Classical grammar remains neutral, like the paint on the artist's palette.

FROM THE OXFORD UNION DEBATE

HOW SHOULD ARCHITECTURE BE DEVELOPING?

The question before us enshrines an assumption characteristic of our age. We are asked not whether architecture should develop, but in what direction. In other words, we are asked for a theory of architectural progress. This reflects the great difference between the ancient world and our own. Whereas ancient man looked to the past for his wisdom and inspiration, modern man looks only to the future in the blind faith that 'progress' will solve the problems which he himself has made.

Before suggesting a direction for architecture I should like to take stock of our present position. The soil in which we grew was tilled by our Victorian forefathers and fertilised with the humanistic, secular and agnostic ideas which they had acquired from the Enlightenment. Around the middle of the last century there fell a seed of thought into this soil – a very simple seed, yet one capable of the most alarming consequences and proving ultimately to be the most revolutionary force in the modern world. I refer to the doctrine of evolution, and the superstition that development is inevitable. Until we acknowledge the effect of such ideas upon the mind – particularly as clothed in the language of Darwin and Marx – we fail to see the nature of our present problem. For art is the visual transcription of the things that are upon the minds of men.

As a consequence of the Industrial Revolution, we experienced an enormous growth in prosperity. Man was freed from want and enlightened legislators worked for the political emancipation, of slaves, of workers and of women. Scientific knowledge constantly augmented the store of human competence and the old dim light of religion was eclipsed by the sun of Reason. By degrees, it seemed, man was becoming master of his material circumstances and in this mastery he found his meaning and his goal. It was precisely in such materialistic terms that the Modern Movement conceived itself.

The belief in progress even made itself felt through the medium of Romantic poetry. In Locksley Hall Tennyson depicts one rising from his personal sorrows to confront a vision of the future, in which 'the war drums throb no longer and the battle flags are furled'. Solace comes to him with the thought that:

> . . . through the ages one increasing purpose runs
> And the thoughts of man are widened with the
> progress of the suns.

The belief in progress, thus elevated from the material to the spiritual sphere, seized hold of the popular imagination. It was translated at last into a kind of universal law; a law controlling every sphere of thought and enslaving the realms of religion, art, music and architecture.

The first effect of this way of thinking was to cause people to reject all time-honoured practices. In architecture the rules of traditional Classicism gave way to a succession of experiments, as though architecture should pursue the unexpected in the same way as science. All at once we find the most remarkable changes in the art of building. For example, the plan of a house which used always to be symmetrical with the front door in the centre, was revised in favour of wilfully asymmetrical layouts with the main entrance at the side or back. The windows – which almost always used to be vertical sliding sashed, placed in the most obvious position for the purpose of lighting the rooms beyond them – were replaced by bays, with large sheets of glass bulging outwards from the facade. This development, motivated by technological change rather than aesthetic judgement, led at last to the picture window – for that is the direction which 'progress' dictates.

In old work the roofs were always pitched from a simple rectangular plan. This was soon replaced by a complicated system of bays, valleys, hips and ridges, which was further 'developed' (following the advent of asphalt and roofing felt) into the notorious flat roof, which, incidentally, bears a guarantee no longer than that of a refrigerator. The walls of all traditional buildings were made in solid load-bearing brick or stone, with lime mortar. Although the Victorians used these materials, the burning desire for change soon destroyed their authority; the wall was then 'developed' into a frame of concrete or steel to be veneered with brick, plastic, or whatever other material should take the architect's fancy.

Most important of all was the rejection of the Classical Orders. Traditional buildings had expressed their personality (which was also a kind of good-mannered conformity) through the use of the three Orders: Doric, Ionic or Corinthian. The Victorians for a short time replaced the Orders with the debased and vulgar excesses of the Gothic Revival. This in turn soon gave way to the doctrinaire conviction that encrustation is nothing but meaningless ornament. All detail thereafter became vestigial and was eventually done away with as an impurity and an irrelevance.

It now seems self-evident that those changes were not really improvements: they were part of a scission in the lifeline of traditional architecture. They erupted into architectural thought with all the violence of conquest: conquest by an alien culture, fired by a new and zealous faith. It may sound a little extreme so to describe the Modern Movement, but let me quote from two of its leading protagonists. First, Walter Gropius, writing in 1935:

> A breach has been made with the past which allows us to envision a new aspect of architecture corresponding to the technical civilisation of the age we live in. The morphology of dead styles has been destroyed and we are returning to the honesty of thought and feeling.

Secondly, Le Corbusier in his great polemic of 1927, *Vers une architecture*:

> A great epoch has begun. There exists a new spirit . . . we must create the mass production spirit. The spirit of constructing mass production houses. The spirit of living in mass production houses. The spirit of conceiving mass production houses. We must eliminate from our hearts and minds all dead concepts in regard to the house.

Such statements demonstrate that modern art and architecture are in no real sense 'developments': they are the visual manifestations of a faith. What posed as a 'development' of the established practice was in fact an ideological attack on it, and one which proved singularly incapable of founding a tradition of its own.

This is not to say that there could not be real development of a kind in architecture. By this I mean a slow accumulation of knowledge, perhaps over a vast time-span, guided more by reverence for the past than by love of novelty. A prime example is the Classical tradition: the line which reaches from the Greek temple, through Roman, Romanesque, Renaissance, Baroque, Palladian and Risorgimento, to the neo-classicism of our own times. The changes displayed in such a tradition are not necessarily improvements, nor are they brought about in a spirit of improvement: they are attempts to emulate what is worthy in altered spiritual circumstances. Change and development involve no sacrifice of principle.

I can point to many beautiful buildings in Oxford: to the Radcliffe Camera, to Hawksmoor's buildings at Queen's and All Souls, to the Gothic and Classical work of St Mary the Virgin in the High, and even to the little Georgian shops and houses along St Giles. All these buildings exhibit great skill and variety in the use of Classical Orders; great wisdom and constructional knowledge in the jointing and placing of stones in arches, pediments, columns, battlements and pinnacles; great mathematical knowledge in the proportion and spacing of triglyphs and metopes in the frieze between columns. They also have a message: they bear witness to a timeless beauty and to a civilised age which is fast disappearing. And yet two or three hundred years later we still use these buildings every day, with no sense of incongruity.

Now compare those buildings with the typical award-winning designs of our era: with the new buildings at Christ Church, Brasenose and Wolfson; with the Florey building at Queen's, the History Faculty building in Cambridge, the Leicester Engineering Laboratory (on which I worked as an assistant 30 years ago), or with the teenage tower blocks in London and Liverpool. These buildings exhibit no skill in the use of the Orders, no real appreciation of mathematics or proportion, no understanding or use of traditional materials; no knowledge of traditional construction. And what do they have in common? First that they have received awards, maximum media attention and endless discussion in all schools of architecture; secondly, and more importantly, that they are all about to collapse. They have failed the test of wind and weather. All the buildings I have referred to leak; all have terrible problems with condensation (in all of them the cladding panels fall off and have to be removed – in one case after less than a decade). One has been seriously considered for demolition and most have been at the centre of prolonged litigation. I am only repeating what we have all read in the popular press. But this is something which we should all take note of: that the most admired and spectacular examples of the Modern Movement are enormous technological failures, despite the fact that they were conceived in a spirit of technological faith. That is why I say that the Modern Movement will lead to its own demolition. Such is the fate of any art that places technique before beauty, and means before ends.

There may be some among you who feel that development, even if nasty, is nevertheless inevitable. I would remind them that the Darwinian and Marxian theories also argued for the inevitability, rather than the desirability of progress. In this way, they encouraged people to abdicate from the crucial task of judgement and evaluation. We have no choice in the matter, they told us, since we are driven on regardless by the 'material' forces of nature and economics. Such theories do not describe the world: they change it. Once they are believed they have a tendency to become true, as people renounce the desire to control their own lives and surrender to the 'forces of history'. This surrender is especially evident in those spheres of life where the utilitarian spirit prevails: in commerce and industry. Our Georgian and Victorian forefathers embellished their factories and offices just as they did their houses. However useful, their buildings also had to be beautiful and fitting companions to the streets in which they were placed. But with the Modern Movement 'economic necessity' acquired a new imperiousness. Offices and factories, since they display our commitment to technological progress more clearly than any other buildings, had to be as 'modern' as possible. Therefore, it is in this sphere that we see what the 'inevitability of development' has amounted to,

and the change in the face of our historic cities is all too evident. London, the town immortalised by Hogarth and Canaletto, is now a city of office blocks: a drab, depressing desert uninhabited at night and by day offering nothing to the eye or the imagination.

Nor is the catastrophe merely visual. The modern ways of building with steel or concrete frame and floor after floor of identical cells, has created its own legacy of psychological and physical disorders. Electric lifts destroy the last opportunity for exercise, artificial light corrodes the eyes, and artificial air the lungs. People are packed into these deep unwholesome buildings like broiler chickens, glimpsing the day only distantly through some window which cannot be opened and breathing the recycled air from a thousand neighbouring lungs. Sick Buildings Syndrome, the disease which causes 70 percent of the workforce to suffer from lethargy, discomfort of the nose and throat, headaches and eye irritation, is most common in the supposedly comfortable 'energy efficient' air-conditioned offices, the principal legacy of the Modern Movement. If you allow yourself to believe that this way of building is inevitable, then you deserve your fate. Alas, however, it is not only the apostles of 'progress' who are destined to suffer from its effects, but also the rest of us. We must therefore break free from the prevailing deception and return to the simple and desirable common sense of traditional building.

How then should architecture be developing? I think it is time that it stopped 'developing'. It should stop in its tracks and look back to the past for wisdom and inspiration. I would go further. It is time, I believe, for some public acts of repentance. What is needed today is not a little more of this, or a little less of that, but a protest against the whole system: not accommodation but defiance – defiance which goes further than the realm of architecture and which confronts the whole culture of permissiveness which is so accurately portrayed in the buildings of our age.

We, the sons of Darwin, conceive of a world which took millions of years to develop and for us 'development' has all but replaced 'creation'. We reject the traditional teaching that God created the world and man and woman for His own Glory. Our only conception of the future, therefore, is one of more and more 'development', more and more 'inevitable' steps along the accustomed path. But has it not occurred to us that the 'developments' of the last hundred years – nuclear technology, the ever-increasing exploitation and pollution of nature, not to speak of those 'developments' in morals (approved or connived at by the recent Synod) – prophecy the end of history and also the end of man? By believing so firmly in our technological nostrums, and by making the work of the spirit subservient to technology, we surrender our freedom and so destroy ourselves. After all, we are permitted to destroy ourselves – and the God whom we have rejected will have us in derision. These are Advent thoughts!

I am not here to talk about Salvation, but about the development of architecture. Nevertheless, as my colleague Richard Rogers has said: architecture cannot be separated from ideology. We cannot think seriously of architecture without raising at the same time the fundamental questions of man's life on earth. Therefore, let me conclude with a piece of serious advice. While we are spared – while the Lord tarry, as we say in non-conformist parlance – let us build smaller and gentler buildings; let us make walls of solid brick or stone; let us roof them with slates and pierce them with sash windows of the kind that have recommended themselves to generations of Englishmen; let us use the Doric, Ionic and Corinthian Orders; and let us take inspiration from the wisdom of our forefathers, so that our buildings will be signs and heralds of a more natural, more stable and more beautiful world.

Taken from a speech given at the Oxford Union Debate, November 1987. Published in The Salisbury Review, *June 1988.*

FROM THE CAMBRIDGE UNION DEBATE
THAT THIS HOUSE WOULD BUILD TRADITIONAL BUILDINGS

I fear that we architects tend to think that the built environment is really the sole preserve of the architectural profession, whereas in fact it is of equal, if not greater concern, to all those involved in the building industry and particularly the general public who use these buildings. The questions that this debate raises are not new; in fact almost every time I am invited to speak it is on a variation of the same theme. At a recent Architecture Club meeting the motion before us was this: 'Vitruvius, art thou sleeping here below? Is there a role for Classicism today?'

When I debated with Richard Rogers at the Oxford Union in 1987 it was on the theme of 'How should architecture be developing?' At Bath recently the theme was 'How can new buildings be erected in historic cities?' One could go on and on, but the reason the same theme keeps reoccurring is that ordinary people are not happy with the new buildings they see around them. It all seems to belie some deep-rooted and perhaps subconscious distrust of all things unnatural which have been thrust upon us by this brave new world of technological achievement. In the last year or two these feelings have been justified by a new awareness of environmental issues. Far more important than any whim of fashion is the question of which way of building is least harmful to our fast disintegrating planet.

I am sure we have all been involved in discussions on this theme on many occasions. Sometimes, lest I should seem too fanatical, I find myself trying to reassure my hearer by saying, 'Of course I make compromises: I don't write with a quill and I don't go to my office on horseback'. Then I wonder why I try so hard to curry favour with the opposition. For if you seek perfection you must study from the past; if you want to perfect your calligraphy you must use a quill; and if you are seriously concerned about the environment and the cumulative effect of high energy consumption, you will long for the day when you can walk to work.

The time is now overdue for us to ask: is it wise to use all the technology we have at our disposal?

We can now design hermetically-sealed buildings, totally dependent upon lifts and artificial light and air-conditioning (full of refrigerants and CFCs and costing the earth to maintain), but what of the cost in global warming and human comfort? We can build 200 storeys high, but what about the infrastructure, the roads and railways, and crime at street level? We can erect structures in stainless steel and reinforced concrete and cover them in a veneer of plastic or curtain walling, but do we consider how to recycle these unfriendly materials when the buildings are worn out . . .

New materials! That's what is always being quoted against traditionalists. I've heard it all before . . . *ad nauseam*. They say: 'Why not move with the times? Why not experiment with new materials and the new methods of construction now at our disposal?' The answer is very simple: these new materials don't last, and the new methods of construction don't produce a permanent or waterproof structure – thus making nonsense of the first and foremost purpose of any building, which is to keep out the rain!

In Cambridge we all know of the plight of the History Faculty Building, and the number of recent buildings which have had to be re-roofed; just a few of the list of casualties of these new, ambitious, hitherto untried methods of building. They call it High-Tech, and it receives high praise and Gold medals from the RIBA but it never ceases to amaze me that an assortment of plastic and steel tubing clipped together around a Perspex-clad frame and leaking at every joint can pose as a great technological achievement. How pathetically all of this compares with any genuine traditional building, with thick masonry walls, properly proportioned windows and a slate roof; or like the Pantheon in Rome with its great brick dome and monolithic marble columns heaved into position 2,000 years ago and still in daily use. That is the technology that should be our guide and the first point it makes is that only natural materials can withstand the test of time . . . clay bricks, clay tiles, lime mortar, stone and slate. Incidentally, these materials cost a fraction of modern materials in terms of energy consumption (compare a stone quarry to a steel furnace). Also, they can always be reused; even lime mortar can be put on the land.

The great thing about traditional building is that it leads inevitably to architecture. If you allow yourself to design within the constraints imposed by traditional materials and construction (and if you are not frightened of the criticism you will undoubtedly receive), you will very soon discover the wisdom of the historic styles, be they Classical or Gothic. Thus we have in this city Perpendicular Gothic at Kings College Chapel; Gibbs indulging in Italian pastiche at the Senate House; William Wilkins building Greek revival at Downing; and a few years later, Gothic revival in the screen at King's Parade. For Classicism is a search for a universally valid form of architecture and, of course, if something is universally valid, it is valid at all times. In this sense you are always doing something that has been done before.

So much for the intellectual arguments; but the general public don't need arguments – they use their eyes, and like the child in the Emperor's New Clothes, they state the obvious. Don't we all know what we mean by an unspoilt village? It is not a village without any traditional buildings but one without any modern buildings.

As I see it, the choice is this: are we to satisfy the short-lived lusts of a throwaway society with their glossy space-age structures, which suck out the earth's resources and leave behind a scrap heap of unrecyclable rubbish? Or do we return to sanity and build slowly and traditionally like our forefathers – preserving our God-given resources for the generations that are to come? If we want a future for our grandchildren, I propose that we build traditional buildings.

Taken from a speech given at the Cambridge Union Debate, January 1990.

THE AUTHORITY FOR ARCHITECTURE
AND HOW IT SHOULD DEVELOP IN THE FUTURE

Until recently it was felt that the Modern style had come to stay and that architecture should continue to develop along Modernist and technological lines. However, in the last few years more and more people have become disenchanted with the appearance and durability of modern buildings and unconvinced by the intellectual arguments which support them. They have therefore tended to look back to see how people made buildings in the past and have suggested that traditional architecture in some form should be a viable alternative to what we see being built all around us today. The argument between Modernism and Traditionalism is debated more and more vehemently and has now become the main issue in the architectural scene. I come to you as a convinced traditionalist having spent all my working life erecting classical buildings and I hope to show you, not only that it is possible to build this way today, but that it is better than the Mod ern approach. I therefore give you eight important authoritative principles from which to look at this subject.

1) Materials. The traditional materials are brick, lime mortar, stone, stucco, slate and timber. The modern materials are cement, steel, reinforced concrete, glass, aluminium, plastics, asphalt, roofing felt and asbestos.

From the technological point of view the traditional materials have one overriding advantage to all the modern materials which is that they remain virtually inert with daily and seasonal changes in temperature. Technically speaking, the coefficient of thermal expansion on stone and brickwork in lime mortar is so minor that it is absorbed within the mass and flexibility of the wall. But the coefficient of thermal expansion on reinforced concrete and steel is considerable, and the figure for aluminium and laminated plastics is about double that of reinforced concrete. In practical terms this means that a modern structure will move with changes of temperature to such an extent that it will crack, unless expansion joints are designed into the fabric at regular intervals (about 20 feet centred vertically and horizontally). This expansion joint must be filled with a pliable material such as mastic in order to keep the structure weathertight. All mastics break down under ultra-violet light and will fail in ten years. In most European countries driving rain beats upon the walls horizontally and enters the structure at the weakest point: the expansion joint. This sets up corrosion to the reinforcement and other adjacent materials, out of sight, and is the chief cause of decay and ultimate collapse of modern buildings. For this reason modern structures have a very limited life. Traditional structures, on the other hand, need no expansion joints and have none of these problems. That is why they last for hundreds of years and can be repaired and re-used indefinitely.

One also ought to consider the cost in terms of high consumption of fossil fuels in the production of traditional and modern materials. Stone and sand only needs to be quarried. Bricks need to be fired in a kiln; but many bricks, like Flettons, are made of shale that burns by itself through the brick. On the other hand, the temperatures required for making cement, steel and large sheets of glass require a very high consumption of the earth's resources and are seriously damaging to the environment.

2) Construction. Following on from materials is modern and traditional construction. Modern construction for large buildings is invariably a steel or concrete frame to which is attached a veneer of walling, be it glass, brick, stone or plastic. These panels are held back to the frame with cramps (again out of sight for inspection).

Traditional construction for large buildings was invariably a solid thick loadbearing wall made of masonry with openings in the wall for windows and doors. The advantage of modern construction is primarily financial, in that it can achieve a thin wall and a very high building which is of great advantage to the developer, by cramming more space on to a limited site. Whereas a traditional building can only really be raised about six floors, because the thickness in the brick wall becomes excessive at the lower levels if the number of floors is increased further. Traditionally, buildings were only raised to six storeys because, before the days of electric lifts, people would not wish to climb any higher. But too many people living and working on too small an area of land causes problems in our inner cities that are insoluble. These towers of Babel inevitably lead to confusion.

3) Windows. A traditional window was designed in such a way that it lit the space inside the room comfortably – it was not too large or too small to make the room either too hot in summer, or too cold in winter. Our forefathers found that a little over one-tenth of the floor area was about right for reception rooms and slightly smaller for bedrooms. The windows were therefore arranged in the external wall in such a way that the rooms were well lit and could be easily furnished. On the other hand, the modern window is normally vastly in excess of ten percent; sometimes it runs from wall to wall and from floor to ceiling. In this way the space inside can be very uncomfortable, hard to furnish and expensive to keep warm in winter and cool in summer.

4) Span of rooms. Traditional buildings generally have a span of 20 feet from the window to the spine wall, making the complete span of the building 40 feet with windows on either side. If you put your scale on the plans of 18th-century cities you will find that all the buildings, whether they are offices or houses, generally have a total span of about 40 feet. This is because they found, by experience, that there was enough daylight to make rooms comfortable up to that span, and it would be unreasonable to expect people to work more than 20 feet from an external wall for light and air. The modern building has no discipline of this sort and often plans vast chasms of space away from the external walls, putting people in working conditions where they can only survive like broiler chickens with artificial air and artificial light. Not only is this not socially desirable for the people who are unfortunate enough not to work near an openable window, but it requires great expense in servicing, burning up the resources of the earth to keep people lit and ventilated in reasonable comfort. Of course, all this high consumption contributes to global warming.

5) Roofs. Traditional buildings always had a pitched roof which was covered with slate or tile and, on very flat pitches, lead. All pitched roofs, if correctly detailed, last for hundreds of years and provide the best protection to the rain. In order to pitch a roof properly one needs a simple plan underneath because of the geometry imposed by the pitches at the hips and valleys. Traditional buildings therefore generally have simple geometrical plans.

Modern buildings tend to have flat roofs covered in asphalt or roofing felt. The life of these materials is very short indeed and is generally regarded as being 20 years maximum before major repair is required. The advantage of a flat roof is that it imposes no discipline on the architect: he does not have to consider solid geometry as he works on the arrangement of the plan and section, so his untidy mind can conceive a building in any way he likes and simply cover it with a flat roof.

6) Symmetry. Symmetrical design is a characteristic of natural objects and is so obvious that it hardly needs to be described; everything that is beautiful is symmetrical. I do not mean that buildings must be identical about the centre line – and in fact, when you study human anatomy you will see that certain organs like the heart and liver are arranged on different sides – but the general physique of a building should strive at balance and symmetry. It is normal to have the entrance hall of a house (or large building) in the centre, with the front door in the middle. In modern architecture all these natural principles are rejected under the specious pretence that it restricts the freedom to design. In fact it imposes a necessary discipline. So many modern plans are really a diagram worked out from the client's brief without being modified and assimilated into a consistent arrangement.

7) Beauty: The Orders. My last two points concern beauty. I have left this to the last because a building that does not have the other ingredients I have just described will never be beautiful. But having achieved these fundamental necessities it is also essential to express them in a way that is easy on the eye. In the past, beautiful forms in architecture have invariably found their expression in the five Classical Orders: Tuscan, Doric, Ionic, Composite and Corinthian. I cannot tell you why they are so beautiful or when they originated, but only say that they are much older than Greece and probably go back to the dawn of history. I do not think it is necessary for one to believe that they were given to Moses when he built the Tabernacle in the wilderness, or to Solomon when he built the Temple in Jerusalem, but it is necessary to believe in their intrinsic merit.

They have an order and consistency of beauty which has always satisfied the taste of civilised men and societies.

Perhaps for this reason, the Modern Movement has rejected all the Orders on principle. There is not one modern building which employs them. The *raison d'être* of modern design seems to be the rejection of all familiar classical principles and forms.

8) Beauty: Mouldings. Beauty in architecture is not simply these Orders but the mouldings that go on them. Not only have mouldings of this kind been developed over thousands of years, as a combination of construction and weathering, but also the shapes have been devised by the minds of men who notice the effect of light and shade and the casting of shadows on simple geometrical solids. Thus the cyma recta casts a hard shadow at the top and a softer shadow at the bottom and the corona casts a shadow right across the bed moulds, but these can be penetrated by the modillions under the corona. It is this contemplative pleasure of light and shade which strikes a chord of appreciation in the minds of those who have eyes to see.

I think we are very poor judges of how our work will look in a hundred years time. It is important for us to realise that Palladio did not try to express his age when he built the Villa Rotunda but thought in terms of a Roman house; and yet, to us, it looks the epitome of the Quattrocento. Similarly, Colen Campbell and Lord Burlington built Mereworth Castle in Kent which was the closest copy they could get to Palladio's Villa Rotunda; and yet, Mereworth does not look like Italy or the 15th century but the epitome of 18th-century England. Somehow or another, whether it is the materials, the brief from the client, or the way we detail our mouldings and weatherings, the age and the national characteristics always find their way into the end result. I have no doubt at all that my work will look like late 20th-century English Classicism.

Taken from a speech given at the Jan Hus Educational Foundation, Czechoslovakia, October 1989.

ARCHITECTURE AND THEOLOGY

My subject is architecture and theology, or rather Art and Faith, the place where architecture and religion meet. The two great authorities on this subject from the last century were Pugin, who designed the Houses of Parliament, and Ruskin, the celebrated artist and writer. Both started their lives as devout Christians, and ended their days in a mental asylum. Perhaps this is a warning to tread carefully and not to expect too much from Art, and certainly not to look to Art for the supreme truth and consolation that Faith alone provides.

These two subjects – music, architecture, and the other fine arts on the one hand, and theology and Christian doctrine on the other – can be compared to two great rivers springing from different sources, meandering through similar territory, sometimes flowing along the same course, sometimes flowing in opposite directions, and then running out to different seas.

In Old Testament times the fine arts formed an integral part of worship. When Moses went up to Mount Sinai and received the Commandments, he was also given a specification of the Tabernacle complete with its dimensions, its division into Outer Court, the Holy Place and Holy of Holies. In addition he was given precise information about the furniture, the priesthood and their vestments, and even a recipe for the incense to be used in their services. He received details about sacrifices and a calendar of special days for feasts throughout the year.

I like to think that in this Tabernacle were the original and primitive forms of the three Classical Orders; Doric, Ionic and Corinthian as they are now known. It would seem appropriate that a simple Doric Order should be used for the Outer Court. The Ionic would be suitable for the five pillars at the front of the Tabernacle, its curved volutes like rams' horns symbolising sacrifice. Finally, Corinthian would be the natural Order to be used for the columns overlaid with gold which divide the Holy Place from the Holy of Holies.

This small but highly ornate ancient building was extremely important for it was initiated and commissioned by God. The design and construction were entrusted to Moses, but the artwork was carried out by two of the greatest artists the world has ever known whose names are given as Bezaleel and Aholiab. These two men must have been a kind of Raphael and Michelangelo to the ancient world and it is significant that the first reference to a man being filled with the Spirit of God, is to these two artists:

> God has filled them with the Spirit of God in wisdom, in understanding, in knowledge, and in all manner of workmanship; to devise curious works, to work in gold and in silver and in brass and in the cutting of stones, to set them, and in carving of wood, to make all manner of cunning work. (*Exodus*, Chapter 35, verses 31-33.)

This verse is of great importance. It tells us that artistic ability is a gift of the Holy Spirit; a creative gift from God the Creator.

An artist cannot produce beauty apart from nature; he must take his inspiration from the natural world. We can see something of God in His works: the trees, the animals, the sea, the dry land. We acknowledge His majesty, His power, and that He is the supreme architect. Unless we have some degree of humility and reverence for the Creator, we cannot produce creative work which is easy on the human eye. The two artists of the Tabernacle, Bezaleel and Aholiab, had these gifts in abundance.

When they designed their temple, architecture was the visual image of worship. The two rivulets were running along the same course and the art of building was inseparable from religious practice.

The same plan can be seen in the Temple of Solomon in Jerusalem 500 years later, although for a much larger building, in stone. It was the envy of the ancient world and copied by the surrounding nations. After destruction it was rebuilt again and again. It was so firmly fixed in the mind of the Jews, that the condition of their Temple mirrored the state of the nation. The people felt that all hope had gone when the Temple was destroyed and when the Temple was rebuilt the nation was revived. It was inconceivable to the Jews of this time that God should speak to his people outside the framework of this architecture. The rivulets of Faith and Art were still flowing along the same bed and the river bed was now wider and deeper.

A few islands began to appear in this wide river, islands of protest and dissent against the force of the current. Chief among them was King Solomon himself. Even at the dedication of the Temple, he says:

> But will God indeed dwell on the earth? Behold, the heaven and heaven of heavens cannot contain thee; how much less this house that I have builded. (*I Kings*, Chapter 8, verse 27.)

Already in those early days, even Solomon realised that there was much that was imperfect about the most magnificent building. This must have encouraged him to think that there would, one day, be a clearer and better way.

Another island of protest was the prophets, who spoke up when they saw the moral state of those who were most zealous for this architecturally orientated worship. For all its art and architecture and music, for all its priesthood and liturgy and sacrifices, the pomp and splendour of the Temple could not satisfy the conscience or answer the deeper longings of an enlightened soul.

In New Testament times, the truths that lay concealed in the Old Testament were revealed in the New. Now it seems the two rivers divide and run in opposite directions. It is hard for us, brought up in a Christian culture nearly 2,000 years after the event, to realise the extent of the change, the mental readjustment required by the work and words of this carpenter of Nazareth. The things he said were completely against the spirit of the times. He took materialism out of Temple religion and replaced it with metaphor. Until he came, the whole concept of worship was neatly confined to particular buildings on particular days and organised by particular people. All this he seemed to turn upside down when he uttered those memorable words: 'I will destroy this temple and build it again in three days.'

Such was the devotion of the priests to the Temple, that this statement was quoted at his trial and accepted as sufficient grounds for execution. Could we argue, I wonder, that a misguided love of architecture was the justification offered for the crucifixion? Architecture had now come close to worship and dangerous currents are formed when the two rivers intersect.

It was left up to the Apostles to reveal the full extent of the destruction and rebuilding to which Christ referred. Their task was to replace the image of worship as an activity confined by the dead stones of a building, to an image of worship in Spirit and Truth surrounded by the living stones of like-minded people. This metaphor was to be repeated again and again by the Apostles, and I will give but two examples here:

> Know ye not that ye are the Temple of God and that the Spirit of God dwelleth in you. If a man defile the Temple of God, him shall God destroy; for the Temple of God is holy, which Temple ye are. (*I Corinthians*, Chapter 3, verse 16.)

The word Temple, repeated no less than four times in this one verse, is used each time as a metaphor.

The Apostle Peter also has a long section about temple building when he says:

> Ye also as lively stones are built up a Spiritual House, a Holy Priesthood, to offer up Spiritual sacrifices, acceptable to God by Jesus Christ. (*I Peter*, Chapter 2, verse 5.)

Peter is not thinking of rebuilding the Temple in Jerusalem made of thousands of dead stones, but of re-erecting a Temple made of thousands of believers.

The Letter to the Hebrews explains in unanswerable terms how all the old Temple worship was a type of Christ; that as the great archetype has come, all the shadows must fade away. It is fair to say, however, that anyone who seriously and without prejudice studies these apostolic letters, will conclude that physical buildings played no part in the New Testament Church.

There is further evidence from our knowledge of language. The Greek word used in the New Testament for 'Church' is 'ecclesia', from which we have our word 'ecclesiastic'. It comes from two words 'ek' meaning 'out of' and 'ecclesia' meaning 'called'. It therefore describes a gathering of 'called out' people. The word is used 109 times in the New Testament, but never does it refer to a physical building. Also the word 'edify' comes from the Latin 'aedificare', meaning 'to build'. It is used 20 times in the New Testament and always means building up in knowledge, not building a structure. Our rivers are now running in opposite directions.

Has the art of architecture ceased now it has lost its spiritual meaning? Not at all! The gospel was spreading without the shell of architecture and similarly, temple architecture was spreading to all types of building – markets, sports stadia, government buildings, private houses – without the straitjacket of religion. To the Christian all secular work is holy; all service to man is service to Christ; and all buildings should honour the Lord: 'The earth is the Lord's and the fulness thereof.'

Looking at history up to the beginning of this century we see a re-occurrence of Old and New Testament attitudes: both worship centred on a building, and worship where the building has no significance.

In the age of the Church's growth, there were no official church buildings at all up to the time of Constantine (AD 330). Thereafter, with toleration, buildings were erected called Churches, for the preaching of the Word and administration of the Sacraments. Some were little more than sheds to keep out wind and weather; some were converted pagan temples with second-hand columns from other buildings (Early Christian and Byzantine epoch). But in time this simple worship requiring a high degree of knowledge and understanding, gave way to more tangible and visible forms, and buildings became gradually more complicated as the gospel became less clear.

By 1500, all over Christendom there were large and impressive religious buildings erected on the Old Testament pattern. These were almost identical in function to the Temple. There were the daily sacrifices at the altar; the priesthood in all its hierarchy complete with vestments, incense, choirs, music, art and Holy Days. The rivers were running together again. But whereas in Old Testament times this type of worship had divine sanction, now with the coming of Christ, it had none. The church of Christ had recreated the temple which Christ had destroyed; reintroducing a priesthood and a sacrifice that Christ had superseded, all as if Christ had not yet come.

This went on until the Reformation, when the New Testament was rediscovered. But architecture was slow to change, since it was easy to convert these buildings to the new and simple service. Only later did the preaching box plan of the Wren churches evolve, thereby introducing a very different type of architecture to that of the Middle Ages. However, after the Reformation came the Counter-Reformation in Europe; while much later in England the 19th-century Oxford Movement pulled architecture back to its Old Testament form.

All this is clearly demonstrated in many English parish churches including my own in Dedham. Almost certainly there would have been a simple brick or wooden church there before 1492. (Wycliffe and his Lollards were active up and down the country and in East Anglia.) But with the power of the medieval church and the riches of the wool merchants, it must have been decided to erect an impressive stone building with nave, aisles and chancel. It would have had a rood-screen across the chancel steps to separate the laity from the priests, who would be up at the east end near a stone altar. In the roof structure were corbels carved with angels heads and over the large entrance door were intricately carved panels with saints in niches. The image of God was no longer engraved in the hearts of the faithful meditating upon the Bible, but carved in wood and stone for an easier, less cerebral, but highly visual adoration.

During the Puritan era the stone altar was replaced with a wooden table. The Ten Commandments, Lord's Prayer and Apostles' Creed were clearly painted at the east end. A wooden pulpit was placed in the middle surrounded by box pews, and in the windows there was clear glass. Any human form which could cause idolatry was removed. Thus the English parish church was brought to its familiar 17th-century form. Although the Puritans cleared the building of these things, they did not destroy it or move the congregation to a shed. This building was part of their culture; it reminded them of the divine attributes of order and privilege and raised their spirits as only art can do. As long as the building was not regarded as a means of Grace it remained harmless to their souls.

But history moved on and in the last century, 'the saints that went out of the door at the Reformation, came in at the windows'. There were numerous images in stained glass; the concept of the altar was replaced; the Ten Commandments were covered by damask curtains and surrounded by a stone reredos with more images of angels; a choir vestry was added in High Gothic design. The visual effect of Cranmer's simple Anglican service was cathedralised, so that a surpliced choir could process behind a brass cross. No wonder the thinking world is confused by what it sees.

In conclusion, I offer some thoughts on our 20th-century position. It seems that our river is nearing the end of its course and has become a wide delta of confusion. I believe that we are now involved in the final crisis that confronts the world and that this is leaving a devastating effect on our minds and hearts.

Up until a hundred years ago, everything carried on more or less as it had since the Creation. The horse pulled the cart and ploughed the field; the wind filled the sails of the boats that transported our goods; there was a modest use of the earth's resources and all waste was naturally recycled. Whether he liked it or not mankind had to live close to his Maker.

But now everything has changed. We are the victims of a voracious technology, ruthlessly consuming the resources of the earth. A Pandora's box has opened which no one can close. Everyone realises that for all their benefits these things will bring about huge collective disasters. The march of progress has crushed gentler species of animal and plant to extinction beneath its feet.

But the gentlest and rarest species are the creative gift of art and the fear of the Creator; both of which, speaking generally, have disappeared. 'The fear of the Lord is the beginning of wisdom'; we have lost this fear and so we have become foolish.

I do not know how to explain this phenomenon, except by relating this lack of creative gift to the Creator. The building of the Tabernacle showed that when mankind rejects the belief in the Creator, then his creative ability disappears. Never before in the history of the world has man been able to reject God so completely and successfully.

Even the Ancient Roman at his most evil had a fear of God which we have discarded. He realised that his life depended on the one who gives rain and sunshine. If there was famine he prayed to Ceres, the goddess of corn; if he was sick he brought libations to Aesculapius, the god of healing; when he was childless he prayed to the goddess of fertility; and he acknowledged his dependence on the goddess Fortuna for good luck. But the pride of technological man has no limits, and is infinitely greater than that of his Roman counterpart.

Whereas the heathen feared the creator and bowed down to wood and stone, modern man fears no God and has no hope beyond technology. Ancient man harnessed nature and expressed this in his art; modern man finds himself tragically opposed to nature and has expressed this defiance in his art. Thus the creative artistic gift must disappear.

This process has occurred in architecture. In the past, we were confined to the disciplines of natural materials – brick, stone, timber, slate and stucco. My own village is a good example. The height was controlled by our ability to climb stairs and the depth was controlled by natural light and air. In our cities the same disciplines applied. But now steel, glass, concrete and plastics, electric lifts, artificial light and air, have given us an unbridled and unlimited freedom which we are unable to control. Cheaper, temporary construction and maximum profit have become our gods. In the 18th century Canaletto painted a view of the city of London from Somerset House. It was a beautiful city with St Paul's dominating the skyline. Today the same view shows St Paul's dwarfed by the new temples of Mammon: the banks which live off usury and the insurance companies which fix their stakes on our misfortunes. In the old days people built as Hawksmoor built in Oxford's Radcliffe Camera. Nobody can fail to notice the exquisite proportions, the genial use of the Classical Orders, the natural materials, human scale and accomplished harmony and how it fits in with its surroundings. Today we build skyscrapers which look like oil refineries eschewing natural materials, working with no sense of proportion and with no harmony or grace. Buildings like these cannot be compared with the buildings of our forefathers. The ability to design and build beautiful buildings has ceased.

Likewise, it is instructive to compare an artist like Mantegna, whose subtle feeling for anatomy, colour, perspective and composition lifts and cheers the soul, with an artist like Bacon, who paints without real beauty, denying perspective and grace, so that all is an insult to the human form. The ability to paint, speaking generally, has ceased. Perhaps the final statement of nihilism is a work like Yves Klein's blue rectangle selling for a vast sum. Who, I wonder, is taken in by these emperors' new clothes? The people who run the galleries, the institutions, the academies and the media, regard the work of Bacon, Rothko and Klein as great art, rather than as what it is: the expression of emptiness; of an age which is morally and spiritually bankrupt; of a world that knows not what to do, nor where to turn.

So is our position today without hope? Are we of all men the most miserable? By no means! As in theology, so in architecture, there is always a remnant whose sights are fixed on another world. And as we toil below, through this short and uncertain earthly life, we can at least attempt to recreate something of His Creation. Every commission, however small, is an opportunity to keep the lamp of traditional architecture flickering and is a chance not only for the architect, but also for the workman, to practise the skills he was born to use: to create with his hands the thing that is good, be it a Corinthian capital in stone or a scroll in an iron railing, or a leaf carved in wood or even a fine rubbed arch in a brick wall. All these raise a man from a mere wage earner to a craftsman:

> Who lest all thought of Eden fade
> Bringst Eden to the Craftsman's brain
> Godlike to muse o'er his own trade
> And manlike to stand with God again.

And though in our fallen state we do dimly grope after perfection, it is this quest for beauty that makes both their work and mine so worthwhile. As in theology, so in architecture. However, it is necessary to bear all the ridicule and scorn that are deployed by the high priests of a cynical and faithless establishment, poisoned by the Darwinian misconception that evolution and progress are mandatory. We are coerced into believing that every age must bring something new. But here again, as in theology, so in architecture – there is nothing new worth having. As Solomon said:

The thing that hath been is that which shall be, and that which is done is that which shall be done and there is no new thing (worth having) under the sun. Is there anything whereof it may be said, See this is new? It hath already been before us in old times. (*Ecclesiastes*, Chapter 1, verses 9-10.)

BUILDINGS AND PROJECTS

1973

ST MARY'S CHURCH, PADDINGTON GREEN, LONDON.
Site works, railings and gates.

WESTGATE HOUSE, DEDHAM, ESSEX.
For Christopher Davies, Esq. Addition.

DEVEREUX FARM, KIRBY-LE-SOKEN, ESSEX.
For JW Eagle, Esq. Addition.

CRAIG-Y-BWLA, CRICKHOWELL, POWYS.
For George Williams, Esq. New bridge and summerhouse.

BROOK HOUSE, WALSHAM-LE-WILLOWS, SUFFOLK.
For Lord Cayzer. Alterations, restoration and garden seats.

HOUBRIDGE HALL, GREAT OAKLEY, ESSEX.
For EB Cooper, Esq. Re-roofing.

SPRING FARM, WIX, ESSEX.
For JAR Cooper, Esq. Re-roofing.

1974

ST MARY'S CHURCH, PADDINGTON GREEN, LONDON.
New organ and case.

WEST WYCOMBE PARK, BUCKINGHAMSHIRE.
For Sir Francis Dashwood Bt. New cricket pavilion.

THE PEDIMENT, AYNHO, NORTHAMPTONSHIRE.
For Miss Elizabeth Watt. Miscellaneous works.

OLD HALL FARM, HEMINGSTONE, SUFFOLK.
For Dan Neuteboom, Esq. New addition.

NO 1 HIGH STREET, DEDHAM, ESSEX.
For Mrs Raymond Erith. Repairs.

1 ALWYNE VILLAS, CANONBURY, LONDON.
For Mr and Mrs John Salusbury. New addition.

ARCHENDINES FARMHOUSE, FORDHAM
CAMBRIDGESHIRE.
For Arthur Evans, Esq. New flat.

BELL COTTAGE, DEDHAM, ESSEX.
For LH Thomas, Esq. Restoration.

1975

WEST GREEN HOUSE, HAMPSHIRE.
For Lord McAlpine of West Green. New column, nymphaeum, bridge, grotto, seat, Doric lodge, birdcage and other garden works.

ST JOHN'S CHURCH, GREAT HORKESLEY, ESSEX.
New addition.

DORKING TYE HOUSE, BURES, ESSEX.
For Ian Swan, Esq. Restoration and extension.

GOLDENFERRY FARM, WIX, ESSEX.
For JAR Cooper, Esq. Re-roofing and general repairs.

1976

CHARLTON, OXFORDSHIRE.
Tombstone of the 2nd Earl of Birkenhead.

OLD COTTAGE, BRADENHAM, BUCKINGHAMSHIRE.
For the National Trust. Alterations.

OLD RECTORY, LAMARSH, SUFFOLK.
For DM Anderson, Esq. Extension and garden work.

ST MARY'S CHURCH, PADDINGTON GREEN, LONDON.
New church hall.

ST PANCRAS OLD CHURCH, LONDON.
Restoration.

NETHER HALL, BRADFIELD, ESSEX.
For the Hon Richard Seebohm. Repairs.

BROOK COTTAGES, DEDHAM, ESSEX.
For Mrs Raymond Erith. Restoration.

THATCH COTTAGE, WIX, ESSEX.
For JAR Cooper, Esq. New addition.

1977

WAVERTON HOUSE, NEAR MORETON-IN-MARS
GLOUCESTERSHIRE.
For Mr and Mrs Jocelyn Hambro. New house.

NO 4 FROG MEADOW, DEDHAM, ESSEX.
For BR Winch, Esq. New house.

SPEARINGS SHOP, DEDHAM, ESSEX.
New side door.

LITTLE MISSENDEN CHURCH, BUCKINGHAMSHIRE.
New extension.

THE DOWER HOUSE, LITTLE ROYDON, KENT.
For the Hon David McAlpine. New doorcase. Pope's seat. Fountain
and other garden works.

NO 4 CHRISTOPHER ROAD, NORWICH, NORFOLK.
For Mr and Mrs John Perowne. Repairs.

ORANGERY AT MAMHEAD, DEVON.
For Michael Szell, Esq. Restoration work.

OLD RECTORY, EAST BERGHOLT, SUFFOLK.
For Mr and Mrs Rex Cooper. Re-roofing.

1978

HOUSE IN EAST LANE, DEDHAM, ESSEX.
For Messrs Baalham and Payne (Builders).

SHERMANS HALL, DEDHAM, ESSEX.
For the National Trust. Restoration and new urn in niche.

BENTLEY FARM, HALLAND, EAST SUSSEX.
For Mrs Gerald Askew. New veranda.

WAVERTON STUD, MORETON-IN-MARSH
GLOUCESTERSHIRE.
For Mr and Mrs Jocelyn Hambro. New semi-detached cottages.

No 3 BROOK COTTAGES, DEDHAM, ESSEX.
For Mrs TC Traill. Restoration.

ST PANCRAS OLD CHURCH, LONDON.
Restoration Phase II.

1979

NEWFIELD HOUSE, MICKLEY, RIPON, YORKSHIRE.
For Mr and Mrs Michael Abrahams. New house.

WEST HILL, COPDOCK, SUFFOLK.
For GF Harris, Esq. Repairs.

CHEMIST'S SHOP, DEDHAM, ESSEX.
For J Phillips, Esq. Alterations and new addition.

HEWITT HALL, DEDHAM, ESSEX.
Classroom extension.

DEDHAM CHURCH, ESSEX.
Quinquennial and repairs.

NO 1 SOUTH SQUARE, GRAY'S INN, LONDON.
For the Honorable Society of Gray's Inn. Rebuilding.

NEWTON HOUSE, FRISTON, SUFFOLK.
For Mrs CMJ Hartley. Restoration.

EAST HOUSE, EAST LANE, DEDHAM, ESSEX.
For Mr and Mrs AW Regan. Repairs.

CUTLERS GARDENS, LONDON.
For Greycoat Estates Ltd. Gate piers and railings.

QUEEN'S COLLEGE, OXFORD.
Redecoration of chapel.

ASHFIELD HOUSE, LANGHAM, ESSEX.
For Mr and Mrs Drysdale. Restoration and new porch.

NO 14 SOUTH SQUARE, GRAY'S INN, LONDON.
For JA Kemp, Esq. Alterations.

1980

THE OLD GRAMMAR SCHOOL, DEDHAM, ESSEX.
For Michael Ivan, Esq. Restoration.

WELL HOUSE, DEDHAM, ESSEX.
For Peter Andrew, Esq. New dormer windows and re-roofing.

THENFORD HOUSE, BANBURY, OXFORDSHIRE.
For the Rt Hon Mr and Mrs Michael Heseltine. New summerhouse.
Conversion of outbuildings to estate office and garage.

BENTLEY FARM, HALLAND, EAST SUSSEX.
For Mrs Gerald Askew. New trellis arbours.

FAWLEY GREEN, HENLEY-ON-THAMES.
For the Hon David McAlpine. Alterations to hall.

WESTON LODGE, NR BALDOCK, HERTFORDSHIRE.
For Mr and Mrs Roderick Pryor. Restoration.

PAVILION AT HATFIELD FOREST.
For the National Trust.

SUFFOLK HOUSE, WOODBRIDGE, SUFFOLK.
For Mr and Mrs John Strover. Repairs.

WEST WYCOMBE PARK, BUCKINGHAMSHIRE.
For Sir Francis Dashwood Bt. New Temple of Venus and grotto.

THE SALUTE BIRDCAGE.

BROOK HOUSE, HIGH STREET, DEDHAM, ESSEX.
For Lord Seebohm. Roof and general repairs.

CROCKLEFORD HALL, ARDLEIGH, ESSEX.
For Mrs Kendal. Re-roofing.

1981

STERNFIELD HOUSE, SAXMUNDHAM, SUFFOLK.
For Sir Eric and Lady Penn. New clock and maintenance.

BROOKSIDE COTTAGE, GREAT OAKLEY, ESSEX.
For EB Cooper, Esq. Restoration and repairs.

PRINCEL LANE, DEDHAM, ESSEX.
For Messrs Baalham and Payne (Builders). Two new self-contained cottages.

SADDLERS COTTAGE, DEDHAM HEATH, ESSEX.
For Mr and Mrs David Dow. Alterations to front elevation.

DUFOURS PLACE and repair and conversion of 48-58
BROADWICK STREET, SOHO, LONDON.
For Haslemere Estates.

QUEEN'S COLLEGE, OXFORD.
Doors to Front and Back Quadrangles. Repairs to pediment and portico to Front Quadrangle.

NOS 10 and 12 THE GREEN, DUXFORD, CAMBRIDGESHIRE.
For Mrs George Glossop.

TURBAN DEVELOPMENT, WOODBRIDGE, SUFFOLK.
Restoration of front elevation and new colonnade.

FARNBOROUGH DOWNS FARM, BERKSHIRE.
For Mr Adrian and the Hon Mrs White. New house.

BENGAL HOUSE AND MUSEUM BUILDING, CUTLERS
GARDENS, LONDON E1.
For the Standard Life Assurance Company. Restoration.

SHRUBS FARM, LAMARSH, SUFFOLK.
For Mr and Mrs Robert Erith. Restoration of barn.

BOAT HOUSE, BRIDGES FARM, DEDHAM, ESSEX.
For the National Trust. Repairs.

HIGHAM LODGE, HIGHAM, SUFFOLK.
For Major Gurney. New bookcase and general repairs.

EAST AND WEST SUNNEDON, COGGESHALL, ESSEX.
For Miss Rose. Repairs.

1982

THE HERMITAGE, DORSET.
For Francis Egerton, Esq. New house.

OLD DEANERY, ST PAUL'S, LONDON.
For Haslemere Estates. New gates.

MERKS HALL, GREAT DUNMOW, ESSEX.
For Mr and Mrs Richard Wallis. New house.

QUEEN'S COLLEGE, OXFORD.
Stone restoration of Back Quadrangle.

DEDHAM HALL, DEDHAM, ESSEX.
For Mr and Mrs Slingo. Conversion of barn.

RIVERVIEW HOUSE, BRUNDALL, NORWICH, NORFOLK.
For Lord Blake. Restoration.

WEST GREEN HOUSE, HAMPSHIRE.
For the National Trust. Rebuilding and repairs following fire damage.

1983

NOS 11, 12 and 13 KENT TERRACE, REGENTS PARK
LONDON.
For the Copartnership Property Developments Ltd, part of Rosehaugh
plc. Restoration.

NEW HOWARD BUILDING.
For Downing College, Cambridge.

RICHMOND RIVERSIDE DEVELOPMENT.
For Haslemere Estates.

NETHER HALL, BRADFIELD, ESSEX.
For Mr and Mrs S Bullimore. Repairs and alterations.

LAWFORD HALL, ESSEX.
For Mr and Mrs Francis Nichols. Re-roofing. Fountain.

SANDRINGHAM COURT, DUFOURS PLACE, SOHO, LONDON.
For Barratt Central London Ltd. Interior of 25 luxury flats.

KINGS WALDEN BURY, HERTFORDSHIRE.
For Sir Thomas Pilkington Bt. Lightning damage and maintenance.

OLD MILL, SNAPE, SAXMUNDHAM, SUFFOLK.
For Mr and Mrs PJ Terry. Repairs.

HOLLANDS FARM, GREAT OAKLEY, ESSEX.
For EB Cooper, Esq. Repairs.

EYDON HALL, NORTHAMPTONSHIRE.
For Mr and Mrs Gerald Leigh. New stables, garage and courtyards.

WEST WYCOMBE PARK, BUCKINGHAMSHIRE.
For Sir Francis Dashwood Bt. New bridge.

1984

NOS 5-8 KENT TERRACE, REGENTS PARK, LONDON.
For Chrysallis Properties Ltd. Restoration.

FARNBOROUGH DOWNS FARM, BERKSHIRE.
For Mr Adrian and the Hon Mrs White. Addition to wing and farm
cottage.

THENFORD HOUSE, BANBURY, OXFORDSHIRE.
For the Rt Hon Mr and Mrs Michael Heseltine. Kitchen garden.

1985

FARNBOROUGH DOWNS FARM, BERKSHIRE.
For Mr Adrian and the Hon Mrs White. New cottage.

BIBURY COURT, GLOUCESTER.
For Mrs Cate Heynes.

NOS 11 and 12 BURY STREET, LONDON EC3.
For Haslemere Estates. New facade.

NEW HOUSE IN VERSAILLES, KENTUCKY, USA.
For Mrs Josephine Abercrombie.

1986

EYDON HALL, NORTHAMPTONSHIRE.
For Mr and Mrs Gerald Leigh. Dairy cottage.

EYDON HALL, NORTHAMPTONSHIRE.
For Mr and Mrs Gerald Leigh. Repairs to main house.

NEW BRENTWOOD CATHEDRAL, BRENTWOOD, ESSEX.

OFFICE DEVELOPMENT AT 16-20 REGENT STREET
CAMBRIDGE. For Downing College, Cambridge.

PIN OAK FARM, VERSAILLES, KENTUCKY, USA.
For Mrs Josephine Abercrombie. Stallion barn, horse barn and
cottages.

BRENTWOOD CATHEDRAL, BRENTWOOD, ESSEX.
New organ case.

ELEVEN HOUSES AROUND A COURTYARD AT CRAWFORD
STREET, LONDON W1.
For National Car Parks plc.

1987

THE NEW JUNIOR COMMON ROOM.
For Downing College, Cambridge.

THE IONIC VILLA, REGENTS PARK, LONDON.
For The Crown Estate Commissioners.

1988

THE VENETO VILLA, REGENTS PARK, LONDON.
For The Crown Estate Commissioners.

RESTORATION TO THE PILLARED DRAWING ROOM.
For No 10 Downing Street, London.

THE GOTHICK VILLA, REGENTS PARK, LONDON.
For The Crown Estate Commissioners.

1989

FAWLEY HOUSE, HENLEY-ON-THAMES.
New front.

REFURBISHMENT OF THE TWO STATE DRAWING ROOMS.
For No 10 Downing Street, London.

THE MAITLAND ROBINSON LIBRARY.
For Downing College, Cambridge.

1990

BRENTWOOD CATHEDRAL, BRENTWOOD, ESSEX.
New Social Centre.

EYDON HALL, NORTHAMPTONSHIRE.
For Mr and Mrs Gerald Leigh. New gates and piers.

THE IONIC VILLA, REGENTS PARK, LONDON.
Alterations and refurbishment for tenant.

1991

NEW FORECOURT GATES AND OTHER WORKS.
For Arighi Bianchi and Company Ltd, Macclesfield, Cheshire.

NEW HOUSE AT PENSHURST, NEAR SEVENOAKS, KENT.

THE MAITLAND ROBINSON LIBRARY INTERNAL FITTINGS.
For Downing College, Cambridge.

REFURBISHMENT OF CHOIR SCHOOL AND RE-FRONTING
OF PRESBYTERY.
For Brentwood Cathedral, Brentwood, Essex.

1992

NEW RESIDENTIAL BUILDING, WEST LODGE GARDENS.
For Downing College, Cambridge.